GIVING HEARTS

Doug Wing

MVHL

For permission requests, write to the publisher, addressed "Attention: Permissions Coordinator," carol@markvictorhansenlibrary.com

Quantity sales special discounts are available on quantity purchases by corporations, associations, and others. For details, contact the publisher at carol@markvictorhansenlibrary.com

Orders by U.S. trade bookstores and wholesalers. Email: carol@markvictorhansenlibrary.com

Creative contribution by Mike Vreeland
Cover Design and Book Layout - DBree

Manufactured and printed in the United States of America distributed globally by markvictorhansenlibrary.com

∕W∕HL

New York | Los Angeles | London | Sydney

ISBN: 979-8-88581-184-2 Hardback
ISBN: 979-8-88581-185-9 Paperback
ISBN: 979-8-88581-186-6 eBook
Library of Congress Control Number: 2025900663

Contents

Special Thanks

I want to offer special thanks to my sister Tina. Her memories and perspective helped shape the characters in this book inspired by our family's real life experiences.

Foreword

Giving Hearts shares an inside-the-home look at the memories and the stories of Hal Wing, the incomparable founder of the Little Giant ladder empire. This book is full of inspiring anecdotes and inspiring examples of kindness that captures the essence of a person worth knowing.

How do you honor someone like Hal? How do you give respect to a man who gave his life providing jobs and opportunities for others? One of the best ways is to breathe life into the footsteps and decisions that drove him to enthusiastically benefit others. These are not just lessons, but they are a window into the soul of a man who changed the world, one ladder and one person at a time. The benefit of reading these stories will hopefully flip on a light switch in your own life as to how you can use your gifts and talents to bless the lives of those around you.

— Chad Lewis - Former Philadelphia Eagles Tight End and author of *Surround Yourself with Greatness*

Prologue

I have been blessed with an extraordinary life and I will ever be grateful for the example of *Giving Hearts* that my parents showed me throughout my life.

This book is written as a tribute to them and their lives of generosity. They never wanted praise and they expected nothing in return. Their lives were spent helping people in unexpected ways and making their lives better.

My wish is that everyone can learn from Evan and Mary's journey, and how transformative life can be when we focus on serving and helping others.

It is truly better to give than to receive!

CHAPTER 1

The Call

M ary carried one-year-old Alison in from the backyard where she and her four children were playing in the grass, enjoying the cool spray of the lawn sprinkler on the hot August afternoon. She noticed the light blinking on their new answering machine as they passed through the kitchen into the living room.

"A blinky light, Alison. Somebody called, but we were making so many giggles we didn't hear the phone ring." Mary made a mental note to check the message once the kids were settled. She placed baby Alison into the playpen and at two-year-old Linda's insistence, put her in also. The boys, Greg, age five, and Marc, age three, followed Mary into the kitchen where she took out a box of blocks for them to play with.

She walked over to the answering machine. I hope it's not the bank again, she thought. I mailed the payment yesterday. We've never been late. She would have considered the answering machine a luxury, but having it meant Evan wouldn't miss out on extra shifts at the grocery store. And they certainly could use the money. The machine had paid for itself many times over.

She pressed play.

"This is David Grimsman from Social Services. I'm calling Mr. Evan Ward in regard to his brother Richard's children. If he could give me a call back at his earliest convenience, that would be greatly appreciated. The number is 555-5309. Ask for Mr. Grimsman. Thank you."

Mary wrote down Mr. Grimsman's number on the notepad she kept next to the phone and set it on the kitchen table to remind herself to tell Evan when he got home.

Of her husband's four siblings, Evan and Richard had never been close, Richard being several years older. He had a good job as a foreman for a company that built high-rise apartment buildings in cities around the country. Those jobs kept him from home for weeks at a time, leaving his wife, Shannon, to look after their three children on her own. Though the family lived less than an hour away, they always kept to themselves and rarely interacted with the rest of the family.

Richard was killed in a construction accident a couple of months earlier while inspecting a job site in Reno. Mary and Evan tried reaching out, as did other family members, but Shannon insisted she could handle it on her own as she had whenever Richard was away on business.

Richard's funeral was arranged by Evan's parents. Shannon had asked for their help so she could focus on the children. Evan's mother had confided in Mary that Shannon seemed detached and emotionless at Richard's death. Mary tried to focus on the positive, explaining that it was just Shannon's way of handling her grief.

"Not everyone shows grief outwardly," Mary assured her.

Shannon made an appearance at the calling hours, and Mary couldn't help but notice how thin and tired she looked. When Mary gave her a gentle hug, Shannon stiffened and pulled back. Mary caught the scent of alcohol on her breath.

"If you need anything," Mary began.

"I'll manage," Shannon had insisted. She left after a few minutes saying she had to get back to her kids. Mary wondered if the kids even knew their father had died. He was away so much and they were so young.

Mary had not seen Richard's children other than the infant photos sent with their birth announcements. Thinking of that reminded Mary that she never received thank yous for the baby blankets she sent. She dismissed it as an oversight by a busy mom. Having four of her own, she could relate, and unless she wrote herself reminders, small tasks were forgotten.

When Evan got home that evening, Mary greeted him at the door with a quick hug and kiss. "Social Services called this afternoon."

"About?"

"He didn't say exactly, but about Richard's kids. We can talk more after you say goodnight to our little munchkins. The last time I peeked in the boys' room

Greg was looking at a picture book. Marc was already asleep. I'm sure Linda and Alison are asleep by now."

"Even if they are asleep, somehow I think they know if I don't look in on them. No matter how hectic or stressful my day has been, seeing them sleeping peacefully makes it all worthwhile."

Evan slipped up the stairs to the small bedrooms while Mary retrieved his dinner warming in the oven. She missed the days they sat down to dinner as a family. She hoped Evan's hours would shift soon. The foil over his plate would keep his meal warm on the table until he came down. Mary knew how precious these moments with the children were to Evan. If anyone was awake, he might be upstairs for a while.

The doorbell rang. Mary looked at the teapot-shaped clock over the stove. We're not expecting anyone at this hour.

Mary got to the foyer as Evan reached the bottom step. They exchanged glances before Evan opened the door.

His father stood on the front stoop.

"What's up, Dad?" Evan asked. "Come in."

His father stepped inside and nodded to Mary. She led them to the kitchen so Evan could eat his dinner while they talked, sitting around the kitchen table.

Evan's father cleared his throat. "I don't want to ruin your meal if you haven't heard—"

"Haven't heard what?" Evan asked.

"Shannon and the kids were in a car accident this afternoon."

"Is everyone alright?" Mary asked, putting a hand to her mouth.

"Klint is in the hospital with a head injury. Shannon had him in the front seat and he slipped out of the seatbelt when the cars hit. The twins are also in the hospital being observed, but they don't appear to be seriously injured."

"And Shannon?" asked Evan.

"That's the strange thing. The man driving the other car tried to exchange information with her and she mumbled 'I can't take this,' and walked off. The police are still trying to locate her. They called me hoping I knew her whereabouts."

"What about the kids?" asked Mary. "Somebody should be there for them." Mary's thoughts flashed back to the day of Richard's funeral two months earlier. She had not mentioned to anyone the smell on Shannon's breath that day, but now she wondered if the accident was somehow connected to Shannon's drinking.

Evan's father continued, "Social Services is involved now. I'm just getting back from taking your mother to the hospital, but the kids barely know her, so I'm not sure her presence will help much. We were met at the hospital by a caseworker, a Mr. Griswald, Grimwald, or something. According to him, the kids are in poor condition, but not due to the accident. It appears they are malnourished and show signs of neglect if not abuse. Those are his words."

"That would be the Mr. Grimsman that called earlier," Mary added.

"I find that hard to believe," Evan said. "Neglect? Abuse? Richard's kids? Shannon? How did we not know?"

"Your mother and I tried to maintain contact, but Richard always had some reason for us not to visit. Shannon wasn't feeling well or one of the kids was sick. They had other plans. Though when we spoke on the phone, he always sounded proud of his children. A few months ago, when Klint turned six, he even invited us to a party, but then canceled a couple days before. A month later, when the twins turned five, we heard nothing, so we mailed cards and gifts." He shrugged.

Evan looked out the window as he swallowed a mouthful of mashed potatoes. "It couldn't be an outsider doing this to the kids. If I know Richard, he would have beat the crap out of whoever it was. So, either Richard was doing this to his kids or he knew Shannon was. Either way, there is no excuse."

"True," Mary replied. "If Shannon was, maybe Richard felt too guilty leaving her alone for so long to say anything. Also, if Shannon was neglecting them, that would explain why it hasn't improved since Richard died. If Richard was doing it, you would think the children would have recovered by now."

"Your mother and I are feeling quite guilty, too. We could have insisted on seeing our grandchildren. Then we would have known. But you know your brother, He wanted to live his own life away from the rest of the family for whatever reason. I've never said this before, but given Richard's rebellious teen years, I was kind of hoping he'd be drafted. That would have straightened him out."

"But with what's going on with Vietnam now, that would have been a drastic measure," Evan said. "We are all lucky in that regard."

"You are so right. I would've had a hard time forgiving myself if something happened to him there."

Evan laid his fork across the empty plate. "Well, if you ask me, Shannon needs to be found now. I can't imagine treating children that way." As Evan's complexion grew redder, Mary put her hand on his shoulder to calm him.

"For now, we don't know the whole story," Evan's father said. "The kids will recover. Let's focus on that."

Mary changed the subject. "What do you say, Ray? Since you're here, how about a piece of apple pie?"

He agreed without hesitation. Mary always noticed how alike Evan and his father were in looks and mannerisms. She tried to imagine Evan being his father's age and wondered if he would be so comfortable with himself by then and not so stressed with financial worries.

That malfunctioning stove burner can wait, she thought. It seemed like a petty worry compared to the situation with Richard's children. She made a mental note to add them to her prayers.

The phone call to Mr. Grimsman at Social Services in the morning would make things clearer.

* * *

The kitchen clock showed 9:00. Evan dialed Mr. Grimsman. Mary sat across the table holding a napping Alison, listening and watching Evan's eyebrows raise and lower as Mr. Grimsman spoke. Mary wished the phone was loud enough to hear Mr. Grimsman. She would have to wait for Evan's retelling.

Evan shook his head. "I don't think that is possible. Have you contacted my other brothers or sister?"

Mary leaned in. She could hear a voice, but the words were not decipherable.

"I will have to discuss this with my wife, but we are not in a position to take on that responsibility."

What responsibility? thought Mary. She watched Evan's brow furrow as he listened to Mr. Grimsman.

"Yes, I will get back to you as soon as possible. Tomorrow at the latest. Good day."

Evan hung up the phone and looked at Mary. She could see the troubled look on his face, one she had become accustomed to as they tried to pay their bills each month.

"Social Services wants us to take custody of Richard's kids until they can locate their mother."

"Oh my," Mary said. "That is a big ask." She leaned back in her chair. "What did he say when you asked about your brother and sister?"

"Dad had given Mr. Grimsman everyone's contact information, and he called. Floyd is still having health issues and didn't want to take on something he couldn't manage. Helen has travel plans with her husband. Sam lives too far away for temporary placement. What can I say? We're healthy and can't afford to travel. Being broke isn't a good argument. Social Services does provide some financial assistance, though Mr. Grimsman admitted it would hardly cover their needs. He apologized several times, but we are the most logical fit. "

"Well, if it's temporary, until they find their mom, I think we could manage."

"You are not seriously considering it?" Evan asked. "Mary, our little house is full already. Where would we put three more kids? And we have no idea what their behavior is like. Do you really want those kids, who are older than ours? What if they have bad behavior? Bad habits?"

"I think it's more likely they will pick up the habits of our children. Don't forget, we're role models too."

"Mostly thanks to you being home with them all day. It wouldn't be fair to you."

"School starts in a couple of weeks. They'll be gone for several hours every day, if we even still have them in two weeks."

"You are such an optimist, Mary. Another reason I love you."

Mary laughed. "I wonder what will happen to them if we don't take them?"

"Foster homes, but they will be in different homes according to Mr. Grimsman. Hard to find someone to take three at once."

"Those poor children," Mary said, adjusting Alison in her lap. "They've lost their dad and now their mom. All they have is each other. I can't imagine our children being separated if something happened to us." She gave napping Alison a little hug.

"You are wearing me down, Mary," Evan said, laughing. "You are right. It's the right thing to do, but only until the authorities find their mother. Let's pray that it is soon. I'll call Mr. Grimsman back."

* * *

Evan and Mary pulled into the hospital parking lot in their old station wagon. Three empty car seats sat in the back seat. His mother, Marguerite, was already waiting by the lobby doors. She agreed to help transition the kids to their new living arrangements.

"At least I'm a familiar face," said Marguerite. "I'm not sure they even know what a grandmother is."

"Or an uncle," Evan added. "Thanks for helping out, Mom."

"The hospital was able to keep all three due to their conditions until we could pick them up. I hope this goes well. Social Services asked your father and I to care for them, but we just couldn't at our age. Even if they were healthy little angels, we just don't have the stamina for it."

"I didn't know they had asked you. As far as stamina, I'm not sure we have enough either. Seven kids in one house. I know some families manage, but seven kids with the oldest being six? I hope we don't regret this."

"Both of you love a challenge. I'm sure you'll make the best of it."

"Thanks for the encouragement, Mom."

"And we'll be here if you need us." Marguerite rubbed Evan's back.

The three made their way into the hospital lobby and rode the elevator to the pediatric floor.

Marguerite put her hand on Mary's. "Don't be too shocked. Klint is six, but he's barely bigger than Marc, half his age. And the twins are almost Klint's height, only thinner if you can believe it."

When they arrived at the room, all three children were sitting on the same bed, dressed and ready to go. Their outfits looked new and draped off them like ill-fitting scarecrow clothes. The children were quiet and wide-eyed. Mary noted that the two boys were in need of haircuts, their dark hair hanging down in front of their eyes. The girl, Hayde, held onto a well-worn stuffed animal of some kind. Mary couldn't identify it from the dangling bits.

Mr. Grimsman introduced himself and then introduced Evan and Mary to the children.

"You'll be staying with Evan and Mary until your mom comes home."

"Nice to meet you," Mary said, smiling. Mary hoped the awkward feeling in her stomach would pass.

While Marguerite and Mary spoke with the children, Mr. Grimsman led Evan to a bed table to sign a few papers. He handed Evan a bag.

He looked in as Mr. Grimsman explained, "Those are the clothes they were wearing when they came in. They should probably be tossed, but letting the kids keep them may be helpful emotionally. You never know."

A young nurse stopped by with another bag and handed it to Mary. "We bought a few playthings for the kids and collected a few of their favorite snacks from the commissary. There are some clothes also."

"How sweet of you," Mary replied.

"I hope things work out for them. I should warn you the boys had a problem with bedwetting when they came in. It's better now, but I thought you should know."

Mary nodded. "I'm on it. I have bed pads from our kids."

The nurse left, and Mr. Grimsman ushered the children to the hallway toward the elevator with the Wards following. They stopped at the nurses' station to pick up medicine and instructions for Klint who was still recovering from his head injury. The bruise on his forehead was a mixture of yellows and purples.

As they approached the car, Mary whispered to Evan, "This is the first time they've been in a car since the accident."

"Good point. We'll try to keep it cheerful."

Mr. Grimsman said his goodbyes and left. Marguerite helped buckle the children in their seats. "I'll see you in a few minutes," she assured them and turned to her car.

The drive home was uneventful. Mary asked questions but got no responses. She wondered about their cognitive abilities. The school will be able to determine that. Until then we'll just do our best. She glanced back. The children were looking out the windows and seemed curious about the world around them. A good sign.

When they arrived home, their boys were looking out the front living room window. Marc was waving a little hand. Mary waved back. She remembered the conversation that morning. The boys were more curious than anything. They seemed to take the idea of sharing their things in stride. The reality may be much different. We'll see. Mary took a deep breath as Evan shut off the engine.

"Our new adventure," he said, turning to Mary and flashing a hopeful smile.

CHAPTER 2

The Adjustment

The babysitter, a high-school neighbor girl, had Greg, Marc, Linda, and Alison sitting on the living room sofa when Mary and Evan entered with their three cousins. The boys held back behind Evan. Hayde clung to Mary's pant leg, which Mary thought was interesting given that they had just met a half hour ago. Hayde already considers me safe.

Admiring the sofa line up by age, Mary turned to the sitter. "You're the best, Jeana. And they all have clean faces." To Shannon's kids she said, "This is Jeana. She's my helper."

Evan tapped each child on the head as he spoke. "Kids, this is Klint, Ted, and Hayde. They will be staying with us for a while." To the cousins, Evan continued, tapping his own children on their heads, "This is Greg, Marc, Linda, and the baby Alison."

Mary wondered what was going on in the minds of seven wide-eyed children as they stared at each other from across the room.

Hayde walked over to Alison and touched her foot. Alison looked at Mary, and when she saw her mother smiling, she also smiled.

"She likes me," Hayde said.

"Yes, she does," Mary replied, sitting on the sofa next to Alison and Linda. She hoped this was a sign of how things would go with all of the children. Alison snuggled on Mary's lap and watched Hayde's every move.

When Greg and Marc climbed down from the sofa to show their toy trucks to Klint and Ted, Mary was struck by the size differences between her children and Shannon's. Klint was barely bigger than Marc who was almost three years younger.

Marguerite arrived with a bag of apples. "I'll cut these up for everyone. The nurse said they always ate the apples." She left for the kitchen.

Mary didn't want Evan to feel overwhelmed lest he change his mind about the kids. Jeana agreed to stay for another hour so Mary could make last-minute preparations. They made arrangements with Jeana to come by for two or three hours every afternoon until school started to be a mother's helper. Mary went upstairs to the bedrooms to put pads on the kids' camping cots they set up for the new arrivals.

Mary had worried about Greg starting school, being away from her all day, but now he will start kindergarten with the twins, so he won't be entirely among strangers. And Klint will be in first grade, just down the hall. Though Mary hoped Shannon would return before school started, she needed to make arrangements for her kids just in case. At first, she hesitated to tell the school about the children's condition and background, but in the interest of helping them, she decided to be up front about their circumstances, also providing Mr. Grimsman's contact information.

The rest of the day was spent getting the cousins settled and fed. Showing them the bedrooms and the upstairs bathroom. Cleaning out and labeling a drawer in the dressers for their clothes.

Marguerite helped make dinner before saying her goodbyes. She pulled Mary aside before she left. "The children seem more relaxed already. They were quite anxious at the hospital."

"I don't blame them. Nurses and doctors and social workers coming and going. Strange noises and lights. And not knowing what's going on with their mother."

"Your home will be a safe haven for them. Bless you and Evan for taking them in. You have big hearts." She gave Mary a quick hug. "Got to get dinner ready for Ray." She stepped outside.

At dinner, Mary made note of the basic manners she would have to teach, but for now, she was glad they were eating well. Linda watched Hayde eating green beans with her hands and tried to copy her. Mary handed Linda her fork and handed a fork to Hayde also. She made a game of picking up the green beans with the fork. All of the children wanted to try it.

"Mary, you are a genius," whispered Evan.

Mary and Evan kept the children busy in the evening by having their two boys show their toys. The plan was to have them so tired out that bedtime would be a short affair. For the most part it worked. Alison fell asleep on Mary's shoulder, so she laid her in her crib. Linda and Hayde got in their beds, Hayde's cot next to Linda's child-sized bed. Mary read them a story about a sleepy fish and both girls were asleep before she finished.

Since Evan was home, he was in the boys' room. It was more crowded than the girls' room with two cots and two small beds.

"Where are bunk beds when you need them?" Evan asked as Mary watched from the doorway. He continued reading a story about a steam shovel. The youngest, three-year-old Marc, was already asleep. Evan's deep voice droned quietly and one by one the boys nodded off. He tried getting up from Marc's bed without making any disturbance but needed Mary's assistance to stand without toppling onto one of the cots. They couldn't help laughing quietly at the situation. Mary turned on the nightlight as Evan turned off the dresser lamp, and they tiptoed down the stairs to the glow of the bathroom nightlight Mary left on.

Now that all the kids were to bed, Evan and Mary sat at the kitchen table, exhausted. Mary poured them each a glass of milk and took out the last homemade oatmeal cookie to give to Evan. She had set that one aside knowing the kids would have eaten every last one. Not that she minded, but Evan deserved a treat also.

"What a day," Mary said, followed by a big sigh. "Hopefully tomorrow will be calmer."

"I was surprised at how much those little tykes ate," Evan said.

"Be glad. They need to grow."

"I know, I know. I was thinking about the grocery store. They let employees buy day-old or damaged goods at a discount. I never took part, but now I think I will."

"As long as it doesn't take the food from those in more need."

Even sat back. "True, but right now, we are the ones in need. Seven kids are a lot of mouths to feed."

Evan ate his cookie, finished his milk and poured another glass. "I was thinking. Maybe I could get a part-time job. Just temporarily, to keep up with the bills. We are just about out of savings as it is."

Mary wanted to protest. He worked long hours already and had little time to spend with his own children, but she had to admit Evan told the truth about their finances.

Evan continued, "I hear they are hiring at the furniture factory. A couple of guys at the grocery quit to work there. I wouldn't go that far. I'll put in an application for part time."

"Just temporary," Mary said.

"Until our finances improve."

* * *

The next day, Thursday, Evan interviewed at Burns-Claybourne, manufacturer of office furniture, and was hired for a third-shift spot midweek.

When he got home in time for lunch, he brought in the bread, milk, and bananas Mary had asked him to pick up on his way. He lifted Alison into her high chair and slid the tray close. The rest of the kids were sitting shoulder to shoulder at the table barely leaving room for Evan and Mary to join them. Evan poured the milk for each while Mary passed out the sandwiches she had prepared. Mary noted how well Shannon's kids were adjusting. She remembered Mr. Grimsman's words of advice. When children feel safe, they can be children.

"This is going to work, Mary." Evan grinned as he told her the specifics of his new job over the noise of the kids' babbling, talking, and eating. "It's only line work, but the company has more orders than they can fill. That's why they now have a third shift. And they are offering higher pay for the night work because right now they have more work than workers. That's also why the foreman is being so accommodating to my grocery store schedule."

Mary took the calendar from the wall and retrieved a pencil from the mug on the counter. Evan always had Wednesdays and Thursdays off from the grocery store. His factory shifts would be Tuesday and Wednesday night.

"Makes for a long day Tuesday, but at least I'll have day time to recover. I've never worked eleven to seven before. I hope I can stay awake." Evan laughed, but Mary sensed a little worry in his voice.

They had not had weekends to enjoy since Evan started the grocery store job four years earlier, but it was not a problem. Weekends were Wednesdays and Thursdays. Now with Shannon's kids and her Greg starting school and Evan working two jobs, there was little chance of day trips even.

It's only temporary, Mary told herself.

* * *

On Evan's next Thursday off, Mary waited until he woke up in the early afternoon to watch the kids before going to the local thrift store to buy some clothes for Shannon's kids. Mr. Grimsman suggested she do so until Social Services was allowed to retrieve items from Shannon's home. Since it was a rental, the landlord would want everything removed by the end of the month if Shannon did not return.

After washing the clothes, Mary took them upstairs. When she opened Hayde's drawer, she found half a cookie under her socks. She took out all of the clothes and found a dried piece of bread and a few lint covered raisins.

Mary's first thought was to remove the items, but she didn't. Why would Hayde do this?

Curiosity led Mary to check under the boys' clothes in their drawers. Both boys had food tucked away. Dried bread and parts of cookies, a few peanuts. Even a shriveled piece of oily cheese. All of these were from meals or snacks she had given the children. How did I not see them hiding their food? If her own children had hidden food in their rooms, Mary would have had a serious talk about attracting bugs or mice and laid out consequences for future incidents. But for Shannon's kids, she felt sympathy.

She looked at the clock. Hopefully Mr. Grimsman is still in his office.

"Social Services. David Grimsman speaking."

Mary explained what she had found.

"That behavior is common with children who never know when their next meal will be. They hide food to keep from feeling hungry, especially at night time. It's hard to get to sleep when you are starving."

"Oh, my," Mary responded, placing her hand over her heart.

"If they get used to a routine of mealtimes, that fear of going hungry will fade. Usually, but there are no guarantees. If I were you, Mary, I would just let them hide food until they don't."

"Yes. That sounds like the best plan. Thank you."

Mary hung up the phone. She found herself imagining the nightmare of the children's prior existence. No child should go to bed hungry. Those poor children. Part of her wished their mother wouldn't come back.

CHAPTER 3

Commitment

Evan took off his tie and threw his white shirt and dark blue slacks into the hamper. He took a deep breath. From one job to the next. He slid on an older pair of slacks and checkered sport shirt. The factory supervisor didn't care what the employees wore on the night shift while they did line work. Still, Evan wanted to keep himself presentable.

A quick look in the mirror startled him. Better shave. He did a quick pass with the electric razor before heading to the kitchen for the dinner Mary set out for him.

"You look tired," Mary said as he sat at the table. He knew she was right. She took the aluminum foil off the plate of food. Steam rose, and the smell of meatloaf, mashed potatoes, and gravy made his stomach rumble.

"I'll get a second wind with this dinner." He leaned sideways and gave her a kiss. "Long Tuesdays mean I get to sleep in on Wednesdays."

"As long as the kids don't wake you up."

"Once we get four of them off to school, it'll be quiet enough to sleep. It would take a lot to wake me when I'm that tired."

"I'm afraid I'll have to wake you tomorrow. I have a meeting at the school about Hayde at 2:30."

"Oh? About what?" Evan took another bite of meat-loaf sopped in gravy.

"It seems she is having trouble with some of her classmates."

"It's kindergarten. Isn't that where they learn to get along?"

"Yes, but she bit a boy on the arm."

Evan stopped chewing and swallowed. "That's new. She hasn't done that here."

"No. Thank goodness."

"That sounds like a mighty important meeting. I'll be up to watch our kids. If I'm not, wake me. And I think I'll call the police department. Find out if there is any news about Shannon's whereabouts."

Mary set out a plate of her chocolate chip cookies for Evan. "It's been almost six weeks. I don't think she wants to be found."

"To be honest, I think the kids are better off without her. I hate to say it but look how much they have improved since we've had them. That Klint has quite the personality. And our Greg seems to be teaching him a lot for being a year younger. I'm proud of our boy."

"I had a feeling our kids would be a good influence," Mary said.

Evan laughed. "And Hayde treats Alison like her own living doll."

"I don't think Hayde was ever around a baby before. I'm showing her how to be a good mom. She so wants to be a good helper."

"She's learning from the best." Evan leaned over and gave Mary a kiss. He stood and carried his plate to the sink before sifting through the pile of mail on the counter.

"This one needs to be paid right away," he said, pulling a bill from the pile. "And this month we can, thanks to Burns-Claybourne."

"We always pay our bills on time," Mary said, "but It would be nice to put a little aside in our savings account."

Evan turned to her. "As long as the car holds together for a while longer, we might. It won't last long, held together with rubber bands and glue, my dad likes to say."

* * *

Evan had settled into a routine at the factory. Check in, put his snack sandwich in the breakroom refrigerator, and watch the clock for his time to start. He was one of three riveters securing the steel legs on the office desks that came down the line. Every few days there would be a different model, but the task was the same. It was pretty mindless work which gave Evan time to think about his future.

He and Mary had talked about having a fifth child, but with Shannon's kids staying with them, another child, an infant no less, would be overwhelming. Of course, if he insisted, Mary would agree to another child of their own, but that would be unfair to her. She would bear the brunt of the additional work while he would continue to work two jobs. They would have to be careful. For now.

About three months in, Evan was called to the supervisor's office when he arrived at the factory. Normally, there was no supervisor working their shift, only a foreman. What's up? wondered Evan. Giving us grief for the desks we flagged last week for the misaligned tops?

The supervisor stood as Evan entered. He was a tall man of about fifty with thinning hair and a wispy comb-over. "Doug Gardner," he said and reached out his hand. Evan instinctively shook it and sat as directed. Doesn't seem like trouble.

Stacks of papers, a well-worn typewriter, and a phone filled the desktop. One of our older models, thought Evan. Every untouched surface was covered in a thick layer of dust.

"You do good work, Evan."

"Thank y—"

"And I have an offer for you. The third shift foreman is moving to the morning shift. We need to fill his position immediately, well, by Monday. He mentioned you as a possible replacement. Interested?"

Evan sat up in his seat. "Yes. Though I need to ask why not offer the position to the employees that have been here much longer?"

"Some guys do the minimum and are happy with that. No ambition. You, on the other hand, seem to want to go places with your life, according to the foreman."

Evan recalled the few chats he had had with the foreman about work ethics and goals. Now he wondered if the foreman was feeling him out for this job offer. *Probably good that I was clueless about his motives.* "What would be my responsibilities?"

Doug ran through a list of tasks, most of which Evan had observed the foreman doing already. "And it comes with a considerable pay raise."

Evan didn't let his excitement show, but inside he was thrilled until he realized the job would be full time, five days a week.

"Do you mind if I discuss it with my wife first?"

"Fine, but HR needs an answer by tomorrow night." He stood and ushered Evan to the office door. "Keep this under wraps," he said, nodding toward the factory floor.

Evan took his place on the line. At this point the work was mostly rote, but his mind raced. *Could I quit the grocery store?* He tried doing calculations in his head but kept getting interrupted by another desk arriving.

When he got home in the morning, he wanted to tell Mary right away but thought it best to wait until the older kids were off to school.

Once the bus pulled away, Evan took a seat in his recliner and watched Alison and Linda playing with stuffed animals on the living room carpet. Marc sat in

Mary's lap on the sofa looking at a picture book. Evan shared the news.

"I've figured it out, Mary. With the higher wages as foreman, working full time at the factory, I will make the same as I do working the two jobs I have now."

"But it will be five days on third shift," Mary pointed out.

"Yes, that will mean sleeping during the day, but it will mean I'll be available during the day when you have appointments or shopping. You won't have to load all the kids into the car all the time."

Evan watched as Mary considered the possibility. Marc wiggled off her lap and sat on the floor with his sisters.

"And It's possible to move to a day shift if one comes open. That's how I got this offer. The night foreman went on days."

"Don't you have to give notice at the store?" Mary asked.

"Two weeks, but I've got vacation time coming, so I'll use that. Well, what do you think?"

"I'll be glad you are not working two jobs, that is for sure."

"Great, I'll stop by the grocery later to put in my notice."

* * *

Evan was surprised that his boss and the owner of Brookside Market, Mr. Brock, were in the store manager's office sitting behind the desk as he entered. He expected only his boss. He took a deep breath and told them his plan to leave.

Mr. Brock spoke. "You're a good worker, Evan. I can understand your desire to do better for yourself and your family. I'm just sorry there are no positions higher up to offer you here."

"Thank you, Mr. Brock." Evan hadn't thought he was even being considered for a promotion. His performance reviews had always been good, but no mention had ever been made. He hoped he didn't regret his decision.

"If things don't work out for you, I'm sure we could find a place for you here if you want to return."

"Thank you. That means a lot."

They shook hands, and Evan left the office feeling a load had been lifted from his shoulders. But a new load was settling in, the responsibilities of being a foreman.

* * *

Days turned into weeks. Evan and Mary had mastered their new routine. Evan would get home and wake up the children to get them ready for school while Mary saw to the younger ones.

The boys had become close and played on the front porch while waiting with Evan for the bus. They jumped off the bottom step to see who could jump the farthest, they watched a bug, they made up silly rhymes. Klint and Ted seemed to be happy kids at times like these.

Hayde sat on the low porch bench and watched the boys.

Evan tried to encourage her. "Would you like to play? I'm sure the boys would let you."

Hayde jerked back a little when Evan spoke, like his voice scared her. I sound too much like her father, Evan thought. Hayde shook her head and pulled her ragged stuffed animal to her chest. She didn't look at him.

When the bus pulled up, she followed the boys.

Evan didn't feel tired until after the bus pulled away. Then his all-night foreman job got the best of him. He was about to wash up and go to bed when the phone rang.

Mary answered. He listened from the kitchen doorway.

Mary turned to see him when hung up. "That was Mr. Grimsman. Shannon is still nowhere to be found. Social Services has started procedures to have the children declared abandoned."

"What happens then?" Evan sat at the kitchen table next to Alison's high chair.

"The children will be available for adoption." Mary said without emotion.

Evan could see the questioning look on Mary's face, the slight furrow of her brow and set lips. Evan was too tired to think through what that meant.

"I need some sleep. We'll talk later." With that, Evan headed to the bedroom.

* * *

Evan woke mid-afternoon to find the three little ones were all down for naps. He could smell the frying eggs Mary was preparing for his breakfast even before he got to the kitchen.

"Thank you, dear."

"Are you awake enough to discuss Shannon's kids?" she asked, flipping the eggs onto a plate with some toast and setting it on the table.

"Sure. What was it Mr. Grimsman said? Someone was going to adopt the kids?"

"Well, not exactly. Since Shannon has not been found, the kids are being declared abandoned. Then they can be adopted." She sat opposite him.

"By who?" Evan asked before popping a mouthful of egg.

"Anyone who qualifies, I imagine."

"Would they be together?"

"Not likely, according to Mr. Grimsman. Maybe the twins would stay together, but there is no guarantee."

"That doesn't seem right."

Well—" Mary trailed off.

"Well, what?" Evan asked.

"Mr. Grimsman did suggest that we consider adopting them."

Evan swallowed his mouthful and set his fork down. He looked at Mary. "You think we should."

"It's not a decision for me to make. We need to make it together."

Evan's mind raced. They were finally on the way to being financially solid. "Seven kids," was all he said aloud.

Alison banged on the side of her crib with her rattle, her signal that she wanted to get up. Mary stood. "We don't need to decide right away, but soon, Mr. Grimsman said."

Evan already knew what his answer was going to be. How could we send those kids to live with strangers?

Mary returned and sat at the table with Alison in her lap. "The children feel like a part of our family now. I would miss them terribly. But I know we have to consider finances."

"Mary, I think you want us to adopt them."

Mary nodded. Her eyes brimmed with tears.

"Well, honestly, I do too."

Mary sobbed softly. Alison looked up at her mother's face and hugged her. Evan wiped his eyes with the back of his hand and cleared his throat.

"But how will we manage?" Mary asked. "Realistically?"

"We'll find a way. We always do."

* * *

On the Thursday two weeks before Christmas, Ray

and Marguerite showed up at the Ward's door with a fresh cut pine tree.

"Grandma and Grandpa are here with a surprise," Evan called up the stairs.

The boys came bounding down the stairs as the six-foot tree was carried into the living room. Hayde, Linda, and Alison sat together on the sofa.

It occurred to Evan that Shannon's kids may not have had a Christmas Tree, but did not want to ask and remind them of their life before. "Let's decorate it right now so Grandma and Grandpa can help."

Mary retrieved the box of ornaments and garland from the back closet and all of the family set about attaching hooks and hanging ornaments, garland, and tinsel until the tree was covered.

"She's a beauty," Ray announced.

"Thanks, Dad," Evan said. "You've made this Christmas special already."

"And we're not done," Marguerite added quietly to Evan and Mary. "The church put together some gifts for the children. We have them in the car. You can put them under the tree later."

Mary hugged Marguerite. "Bless you."

"I know you both have made a monumental decision to make these children a part of your family. We will do all we can to help, and so will many other people you know." She pulled Evan close and hugged him.

Evan felt overwhelmed by the kindness. I wish I could share this feeling.

CHAPTER 4

Rumors

One morning in early Spring, the phone rang in the Ward's kitchen. Evan was coming in the house through the kitchen door having put the kids on the bus and returned the trash cans to their place under the back porch.

Mary sat Linda in the chair next to her and got up to answer the phone.

"Hello?"

Silence on the other end.

"Hello?"

When she was met with more silence, she looked at Evan, shrugged, and hung up the phone.

"Wrong number," she said to Linda as she picked her up and returned her to her lap. To Evan she asked, "A thought crossed my mind. You don't think that could have been Shannon, do you? Maybe she's missing them. That would certainly complicate things."

"I wouldn't be quick to jump to conclusions, Mary. It could have been anyone."

"True," she replied. "The other day, I got a call from a lawn mowing service and it's barely warm enough for grass to grow."

"The early bird gets the worm," Evan reminded her.

"Not warm enough for worms yet either," she joked.

"Shannon must know the police are looking for her. I doubt she would make herself vulnerable to getting caught."

"As a mother, I would want to know my children were okay if I could not be with them." She gave Linda a cuddle. "I wonder if she knows she can't get her children back, that they've been put up for adoption."

"I doubt she cares. If I were her, I would be glad they are someone else's worry now. She obviously couldn't handle being their mother alone after Richard died."

"I wish she knew there were people who would have helped her if she had asked."

"Water under the bridge, Mary. Water under the bridge."

Alison started fussing in her playpen. The conversation was over. Evan headed to the bedroom for some sleep.

That afternoon, Evan and Mary waited on the front porch in the warm April sun with the three little ones, waiting for the school bus to drop off the others.

"I forgot to mention, Mary, that there is a rumor at work that the factory owner, Mr. Burns, is fixing to sell the company. He wants to retire and neither of his children has any interest in taking over the business."

"Will you still have a job if it sells?"

"I imagine so. It's not like there are other people around here that have experience."

* * *

At work that night, the rumors persisted. As the second-shift workers left, they shared what they had heard with the incoming third shift. No sale was imminent. The owner had just been thinking out loud about reaching his sixty-fifth birthday later that year.

But a seed had been planted in Evan's mind. Would it even be possible? Could I raise enough money? Could I afford the risk? While he worked, he thought. There has to be a way.

In the following weeks, the rumors died down. The pace of work increased and decreased depending on the orders received.

On break one day, one of his older coworkers commented, "The owner used to talk about going robotic, but sales would never justify the cost. We're too small of an operation. So, we still do it the old-fashioned way. It keeps us all employed."

That's a good thing," Evan responded.

His co-worker continued, "You know, we usually see a new model or two by this time every year. Now I'm thinking those rumors are true. Not likely to start new designs if you are selling the company."

Evan nodded. "You think he's really going to sell?'

"Wouldn't you? He's earned his retirement, if you ask me. And I heard his health isn't the greatest, so why wait?"

This new information set Evan's plan into action.

* * *

When Evan arrived at home in the morning, he ate breakfast with Mary and the children before getting the older ones on the bus. As soon as the little ones were busy playing on the living room carpet, he explained his idea to Mary.

Mary listened; her eyebrows raised. "I don't know much about business loans, but I can't imagine our bank would take a risk on such a large loan."

"The risk is ours, Mary. The bank would have the business as collateral."

"But would they?"

"I won't know unless I ask. The company has been in operation for over forty years and is well known and solid. I'll call and make an appointment when the bank opens."

* * *

Evan parked his old station wagon a couple of blocks from the Central Bank. It would do no good for them to see the car I drive and make a judgment based on that. He straightened his tie in the car's vanity mirror and stared himself in the eyes. You can do this.

The sun was shining as Evan walked to the bank, but the perspiration Evan felt was not from that. It was the possibility of no that had him worried.

The heavy glass door pulled harder than he expected. He held it open for a young woman on her way out before he entered.

He walked past the tellers to the desk of a matronly woman with cat-eye glasses and graying hair swirled into a large bun.

"I'm here to see Mr. Jeff Spackman. Evan Ward."

"He's expecting you." She stood and ushered him to the office door. "Evan Ward has arrived."

"Mr. Ward. Come in. Have a seat," said Mr. Spackman, smiling and holding out a hand for a handshake.

Evan obliged and sat down in a soft chair in front of Mr. Spackman's desk. He couldn't help but notice it was a Burns-Claybourne model.

"My secretary informs me you are here about a business loan. How can we help?"

"At this point, it's merely an inquiry about a possible future loan. I have to start somewhere." Evan sat straight. "As you may have heard, Mr. Burns may be selling the Burns-Claybourne factory in the near future."

"Yes. Yes. I have an uncle and a cousin who work there. I'm aware of the rumors."

Evan logged that piece of information in his memory. "What would be the best way to secure a loan to buy the company?"

"You?"

The way Mr. Spackman asked, made Evan feel deflated. "Yes, me. I just need to know if it is possible for a person like me to take out a loan to buy the company."

"It is possible, given the right circumstances."

"Can the business be used as collateral against the loan?"

"If that is the route the seller wants to take. Usually, a seller will work directly with the buyer, though a substantial down payment is often required."

This new information was difficult to hear. I have no savings for a down payment. "Thank you for your time." Evan left the bank deep in thought. If it's possible, I'll find a way.

* * *

On the Friday evening before Mr. Burns' birthday, the factory shut down for a few hours so all of the employees could attend the owner's sixty-fifth birthday party at Riverside Country Club, a local event venue. Evan was aware of the rumor that Mr. Burns was going to announce the future of the factory.

Mary and Evan arrived at the party with all but the youngest two children who stayed home with Ray and Marguerite. They were greeted at the door with pointy party hats and blow whistles. Evan helped Greg and Marc put on their hats, while Mary helped Hayde, Ted and Klint. Immediately, the boys began blowing on the blow whistles so they unwound into each other.

"You sillies," Mary said.

It was the largest gathering Evan's kids had ever been to, and he wondered if Shannon's kids had ever been to a big party, or any party at all.

Evan carried a reluctant Ted but was stopped by one of the owner's secretaries who insisted he and Mary put on party hats also. He felt a little sheepish until he saw all of his coworkers in the hall wearing hats.

"Mr. Burns wants everyone to participate," said one of the secretaries as she stretched the thin elastic band under Evan's chin and held the conical hat to his head.

Ted looked at Evan and laughed.

"We all get to look funny tonight, Ted," said Mary as she held Hayde and Marc by the hand and the group made their way to an empty table by the far wall.

Instrumental pop music was playing through loud-speakers, and a few people were dancing in the open center of the large room. The kids sat wide-eyed, watching. Mary walked over to the buffet table and filled two plates with cheese, crackers, and various vegetables for the kids to munch on. When she returned to the table, Evan offered to get plates for himself and Mary.

"Evan, maybe it would be good for you to intro-duce yourself to some of the day shift people," Mary suggested. "You never know when a connection could come in handy."

"I was thinking that very thing."

A waitress brought over a pitcher of lemonade and several paper cups for the kids. "Less spilling this way," she offered.

"Bless you," Mary replied.

Evan left the table as the waitress began to pour the drinks. He joined a small group of men standing by the end of the buffet table. "Mind if I join you? I'm Evan Ward. Night shift."

"I'm Javier Ferro. Night shift, eh? How do you do it? I'd be falling asleep every night."

"You get used to it. You just have to plan to sleep during the day."

An older man, portly and balding, chuckled. "I heard the night shift is for guys that don't like their wives."

Evan was taken aback. "That may be true for some, but not me. I'm hoping to get on days soon." He did miss the end-of-day chats he and Mary had after they had settled in for the night. But this is temporary, he assured himself.

"I wonder when Mr. Burns is going to show up. It's his party," said one of the men.

The group broke up and filled plates at the buffet. Evan was stopped by a young woman in a short green dress and white high-heeled boots.

"You're new around here. I haven't seen you at the factory." She smiled and batted her eyelashes at him.

"Not very new. Night shift."

"I work mornings. I can't believe I never noticed you leaving." She looked down at his left hand. "Married. All the good ones are." She sighed. "Nice to meet you anyway." She walked off.

"Who's the blond?" Mary asked when Evan returned to the table.

"She didn't tell me her name, but what an interesting mix of people working at Burns-Claybourne." Evan was reminded of the collection of people who worked at the grocery store. I guess every place has its personalities.

Mr. Burns arrived a short while later with his wife, two adult children, and their families. Everyone sang a rowdy version of "Happy Birthday To You" while Mr. Burns smiled and waved from the front of the hall.

After the clapping died down, the room grew quiet. This was the moment everyone had been talking about. The big announcement.

Greg tapped his father's shoulder. "Where is the cake?" he asked in a loud voice.

The room erupted in laughter.

"Young man," Mr. Burns said from across the room. "That is an excellent question. Please come up and help yourself to the first piece."

Evan felt embarrassed but walked Greg up to the front. Mrs. Burns gave Greg a small paper plate with a large piece of chocolate cake on it.

"Smart boy you have there, Ward," said Mr. Burns.

"Thank you, Sir." Evan was surprised Mr. Burns knew his name. They had met briefly one time shortly after Evan had been hired.

"Everyone, please join us," called Mr. Burns. A line formed as everyone queued up for a piece of cake.

If there was going to be an announcement, it would have to be later.

CHAPTER 5

Safety

Mary set out the plate of scrambled eggs and toast for Evan's afternoon breakfast when she heard him coming down the stairs. The night shift foreman position was still his after almost a year, but she knew there was no use complaining about it. *This is what must be for now, and I will make the best of it.*

Evan sat at his usual seat and began buttering his toast before speaking. "I'm going to the car dealer today to see about that used wagon. I hope it's still there. When I called, they said they take trade-ins, and I want to get rid of it before we have to sink any more money into repairs. I'll clean the kids' stuff out before I go."

"I know we really need a better car, but remember we made an annual commitment to the church to help fund the Young Men's High Adventure."

"When do they need that by?"

"I received a call this morning." Mary absentmindedly twisted a dish towel in her hands.

"I'll stop at the bank. Maybe I can take out a short-term loan for the car."

The mention of a loan was the opening Mary needed. "Has Mr. Burns made any mention of selling the company lately? It's been months since his birthday."

"According to the latest rumor, he has met with real estate brokers and lawyers. The other day, he walked through the factory with some men in suits during our shift. He passed it off as his quarterly third shift walk-through, but I don't remember him ever having anyone with him before."

"That does sound suspicious." Mary looked at the clock. "Time for the bus."

Evan took the last few bites of egg and carried his last piece of toast with him to the front porch.

The bus pulled up a minute later. The three boys scurried down the bus steps and raced each other to the porch. Hayde took her time and had a scowl on her face.

"What's up, Hayde? Did you have a good day?" Mary asked.

"No." Hayde stomped up the porch steps and walked inside the house.

Mary watched her walk up the steps. "Poor girl. I'll see if I can find out what's bothering her. She's been so moody lately."

Evan shrugged. "She hasn't said anything to me. I wonder if she is missing her mother."

"We're her parents now," Mary reminded him, "but I know what you mean."

* * *

Mary checked the children's dresser drawers every time she put away the clean laundry. There was no food in any of the drawers. Mr. Grimsman was right. They must feel safe about food now.

Hayde, now in first grade, seemed to have adjusted to school, though at the last teacher conference, the teacher did use phrases like somewhat developmentally delayed and below her peers. Her twin, Ted, had a similar report from his teacher, but seemed to be making steady progress and had many friends.

So, it was surprising to Mary that Ted would be the one to have nightmares. Mary woke to loud screaming and moaning coming from upstairs. Without even grabbing her robe, she stumbled up the stairs not knowing what she would find. Shannon! flashed through her mind. The sound was coming from the boys' room.

Seeing that Ted was alone in his bunk writhing and tangled in his blanket, she pulled him to her lap and hugged him. "It's okay. It's okay." Thankfully, he had not wet the bed.

Gradually, Ted calmed without waking and she laid him back in his bed. She straightened the blanket and covered him.

Mary looked over at the other bunk bed and saw Klint sitting up, blinking. "Go back to sleep, Sweetheart. Nothing to worry about." She stood and tucked Klint back under his covers and made sure both were sound asleep before she left the room.

I wish Evan were home on nights like this. Mary returned to her room downstairs but laid awake wondering what Ted had been dreaming about.

When Evan got home in the morning, Mary told him about Ted's nightmare episode. Evan went upstairs as usual to wake the school-aged kids.

Upon his return to the kitchen, he announced, "Ted seemed cheerful and got dressed as if nothing was out of the ordinary,"

Mary set out the breakfast dishes. "That's reassuring, at least. Of the three, he seems to be the one adjusting the best. That's why it seems so strange."

"Maybe the nightmare is his way of handling things subconsciously."

"I hope you are right. And I hope it is resolved."

The boys and Hayde came downstairs a couple of minutes later in a race to see who would be first to the table. Mary had a mind to scold them, but she was thankful, they felt comfortable being normal kids, especially Ted this morning. Mary could not help but watch him for any sign of what might be troubling him.

She followed the same pattern almost every night for the following few weeks, only getting a break when Evan had nights off. It was exhausting, but whenever the thought of not adopting the children crossed her mind, she dismissed it. We're doing the right thing.

She lay in bed, unable to fall asleep. It almost seemed like a different lifetime from when Evan worked at the grocery store, and they had just four children. Evan's foreman job was supposed to help them build savings, but with the need for a reliable car and the expense of bunk beds for the boys, not to mention the grocery, clothing, and medical expenses, they were no further ahead. At least we're not falling behind. Mary closed her eyes.

She woke to Evan tapping on her shoulder. "Mary, wake up. Are you okay?"

Mary opened her eyes and looked at Evan and then at the clock. "Oh, my! I must have forgotten to set the alarm." She sat up.

"It's fine. I'll wake the kids. They can have cereal today. Don't worry." Evan left the room, and Mary heard him head up the stairs.

The next night, there was no nightmare. Nor the next or any night after that. Ted seemed to have worked through whatever issue he had. Only then did Mary realize how exhausted she had been. Mary chuckled to herself. What next?

* * *

Mary didn't have to wait long. The phone rang while Mary was giving the three little ones their lunch. She put a few grapes on each child's plate and answered the phone on the second ring hoping Evan did not wake up.

"Mrs. Ward? This is Bill Philips from Evan's old job at the grocery. Is he at home?"

"He's sleeping. Can I take a message?"

"Ask him to give me a call. I'm hoping he can help us out for a little while."

"I will."

Philips thanked her, and she hung up the phone. They want him to go back to work there. That would complicate things. She wondered what Evan's reaction would be.

Linda followed Marc into the living room after lunch. Mary lifted Alison down from her high chair and she toddled after them. She was big enough now that the others let her play without fussing.

The phone rang again.

"Hi, Mary. Is this a good time?"

Mary recognized the voice. Joyce from the Relief Society at church. She stretched the phone cord so she could see the children playing in the living room. "Yes. What can I do for you?"

"Can I stop by and pick up the lap blankets for the nursing home?"

Mary froze. She had been so preoccupied with the kids it had slipped her mind completely. "They're not ready, Joyce. I can drop them off at the nursing home as soon as I have them finished." She stepped back into the kitchen and twirled the phone cord with her finger.

Joyce sighed. "I was counting on them for delivery today with the other items."

Mary pictured Joyce's exasperated eye roll. She was one of those perfectionists that liked to be in charge. "I'm sorry, Joyce. Things have been a little hectic around here."

"I'm sure they have, especially with those children."

Mary wasn't sure she liked the way Joyce said those. "I've got to go, Joyce. Talk to you soon."

Evan was walking into the living room from the hallway when Mary entered from the kitchen. "You're up early. I hope the phone didn't wake you."

"No. Thinking about work."

"Speaking of work, Bill Philips called. He wants to talk to you about helping them for a while."

"I heard a rumor that their new guy wasn't working out. I hope they don't expect me to go back full time. Even for a pay raise."

"And Joyce called from church. I completely forgot I was going to make lap blankets for the nursing home. I need to buy king-size blankets, quarter them, and sew trim around each one." Mary stopped her description. No need to blather on with details.

"When do you need them?"

"It was supposed to be today, but I told Joyce I'd deliver them myself as soon as they are finished. Maybe I could get your mother to help."

"She'd be glad to, I'm sure. During the war, she used to repair donated clothes at the church to give to the wives and children of the soldiers. Money was tight for a lot of people then."

"I never knew your mother did that."

"Hand sewing or machine, she's a whiz. She used to make many of our clothes too. They looked better than store-bought."

"She's been hiding her light under a bushel, that's for sure. I'll give her a call."

With Marguerite's help, the large blankets were purchased, quartered, and trimmed by the next afternoon. Mary and Marguerite loaded up Marguerite's car. Ray was left with Linda and Marc while the women took Alison with them to deliver the blankets.

Mary confided as she pulled out of the driveway, "I admit, I have an ulterior motive for bringing Alison, The nursing home employees and residents love seeing little ones, and it will help smooth over the blankets being late."

"I don't think they will mind at all, and I'm sure Alison will soak up the attention." Marguerite laughed.

"Being the youngest of seven, she might need some attention focused on her. It's easy to be lost among her siblings."

"I have no doubt she will learn how to get her share of attention. I was the baby of my family. We have our ways, don't we, Alison?" Marguerite glanced back at Alison with a sly grin.

Alison looked up when her name was mentioned.

The drive to the nursing home took the women through a rough part of town. Several people were sleeping or sitting on the benches and sidewalks. Their clothes were tattered and filthy. Their faces were gaunt and drawn.

"It is so sad to see," Mary said. "I wish more could be done to help them."

"It is an overwhelming task, Mary."

"I know, but even small acts of kindness make a big difference."

"Very true. You sound a lot like me."

"That must be where Evan gets it from then."

"I can't take all the credit. His father Ray is a generous man himself. All those years he worked on the railroad he had a ten-acre garden that he tended. He would give away most of what he grew to the needy folks. He said his pleasure was in the growing, not the having. Nature provided the food; he just helped it get where it needed to be."

"Evan has told me about working on the farm when he was younger."

"Ray has had to give that up now due to his health. He has a small patch now for us."

"We all have our time to give, it seems," Mary said. "And our time to rest."

CHAPTER 6

Opportunity

W hen Evan pulled into the factory parking lot, as he did every evening just before eleven, he felt a tugging sense of unease about his future.

Everyone on the night shift was talking about the latest rumor as they clocked in.

Apparently, someone on the morning shift had seen one of the men from Mr. Burns' walk-through last month coming in from the parking lot and heading to Mr. Burns' office. This led to speculations about an imminent sale of the factory. Would they have jobs? Would they get raises? Who would buy it? How much was the asking price?

The sense of unease about the future Evan felt seemed to be spreading.

One of the longest working employees, Larry Thornton, spoke up. "Mr. Burns started this company over forty years ago with Mr. Claybourne, rest his soul. It's part of our community now. I think he'll be looking out for us whoever he sells it to. I don't think he'd do wrong by us."

"I hope not. I can't afford to be out of work. I've got a mortgage to pay," another said.

That sentiment was echoed by many others, including Evan. "I have a mortgage, too."

"And seven kids," his coworker added.

"I wouldn't change a thing," Evan responded in his defense. "Worth every penny."

Evan spent his shift thinking about his fading opportunity to buy the company. Since first thinking of the idea, Evan had taken out a car loan and paid it back early. And he had never been late on a mortgage payment, even when it meant they had to do without a working stove, cooking meals on a hot plate soon after they bought the house, when it was only four of them. His credit was good, but he had no savings to speak of.

After he got home that morning, he helped get the older kids off to school before settling down with Mary and the little ones on the sofa. He wanted to share his thoughts about the new rumors, but with Alison fussing, Mary insisted he go to bed.

"We can talk later," she said.

When Evan came into the kitchen for his afternoon breakfast, Ray was sitting at the kitchen table, eating a biscuit.

"Hi, Dad. What brings you here?"

Ray pointed to a large paper bag in the chair next to his. "Your mother sent me with some kids' clothes she picked up on sale."

"Thank her for us."

"Mary already relayed that request. Now, Mary tells me you are interested in buying the Burns-Claybourne factory."

"Well, the factory and the business."

"Are you sure it's a good idea? That's a huge responsibility."

Mary carried Alison into the kitchen and placed her in her high chair. Linda followed and climbed into a chair next to Evan at the table while Mary set out their snack of crackers and grapes.

"Dad, I'm tired of working and working and barely staying above water. This is my chance to do something big. It's been on my mind for over a year."

Ray looked at Mary.

Evan saw the skeptical look. "Mary supports me on this. We know it's a risk, but no risk, no reward. Isn't that what they say?"

"If you need money to make it happen, I think I can help some. We'll talk if it comes to that."

"Thanks, Dad. I feel like I'm ready for this opportunity. I don't care how hard it is; Mary and I are up for it."

"You make a great team, you two. And before you know it those kids will be employees."

Evan laughed. "Don't rush it, Dad."

"Yes," Mary added, "let's get them all through school first."

Evan sat with Mary and the two little ones at the kitchen table while they ate their snacks. Dad was right.

It seems like yesterday Mary and I sat here with our little Greg and Marc – just the four of us like this. Only now we are a family of nine.

* * *

The man-in-the-suit rumor turned out to be a dead end. Several more months passed and Burns-Claybourne chugged along as it had, though a new rumor circulated every few weeks about a possible sale. Everyone turned out to be false.

Evan was used to the emotional ups and downs, so his reaction to the latest tidbit circulating the breakroom and floor was muted.

"I heard Mr. Burns may just close down the factory if he doesn't get a buyer," Evan overheard someone say.

"We'd all be out of work," said another.

"He ought to lower the price. Then maybe someone would be interested."

Evan's ears perked up. A lower price would make it more feasible to put in an offer.

Mr. Burns conducted a surprise walk-through of the third shift that same night. This time with only one other person. The man appeared to be inspecting the machinery and taking notes. Evan, in the middle of welding, nodded to the pair as they approached his station. Mr. Burns touched his shoulder as they passed, returning the nod.

Evan did not want to wait any longer to make his move. He made up his mind to meet with Mr. Burns as soon as possible. If Mr. Burns is going to lower the asking price, I don't want to miss the opportunity to bid.

* * *

The next day, Evan stayed up after getting home and drove into Burns-Claybourne for the mid-morning appointment he arranged with Mr. Burns' secretary. He looked in his rearview mirror and patted his hair and straightened his tie. *If only I could calm my insides as easily.*

The secretary, a fifty-ish woman with dyed blonde hair pulled up in a neat bun on the top of her head, ushered him right into Mr. Burns' office.

"Well there, young man. Evan Ward, is it? The man with the smart little boy? I remember."

"Yes, that would be me, Mr. Burns."

"Let me introduce you to my secretary, Paulene Greenwood. She has been with Burns-Claybourne since the early days. She has a fantastic memory. So many details I have forgotten. I'd be lost without her."

"Nice to meet you," Evan said, slightly bowing and holding out his hand.

Paulene shook his hand. "Likewise, Mr. Ward."

Mr. Burns motioned for Evan to sit opposite him in front of his large desk. He asked about Evan's family and recounted his own adventures in parenting. "I can't imagine having seven small children. Two was enough for me."

"We are blessed. We have family nearby to help," Evan said. He didn't think about it often, but he was very thankful for his parents' help.

Mr. Burns cleared his throat and leaned forward on his desk. "So, you want to buy Burns-Claybourne?"

Evan was startled at the abrupt change in the conversation, but now they were onto the reason for the meeting. "I see this as a golden opportunity. It's a solid company with a good reputation. This is a great town, and the employees, the ones I know, seem to like working here."

"I like to think we have a positive working environment. It's good to hear it from the floor. But about you, Mr. Ward, what drives you? Why do you want this company?"

"My motivation?" Evan thought for a moment. "I want to do well by my family and myself. When presented with an opportunity to do so, I strive to achieve."

"That sounds like a worthy goal."

"And I know rumors are just rumors, Mr. Burns, but many employees are worried the factory will close down and they'll be out of work. And where would 100-plus people find work in this town on short notice? I would keep the factory open and give my best efforts to make it bigger and better if possible."

Mr. Burns nodded his head as Evan spoke. Evan tried to fathom what he was thinking.

"You should know, Mr. Ward, that I did get an offer for the company a week or so ago for the original asking price."

Evan's heart sank.

"But I turned it down. A foreign firm. They wanted to buy it and close it down and build a shopping center or something. I agree with you one hundred percent. Closing down would hurt this community. I couldn't do it. I just couldn't."

"Thank you."

"You are the first person who is interested in the company that I trust to do right. Let's get down to facts and figures."

They spent the next half hour discussing the details of the sale. Evan would provide a downpayment and Mr. Burns would hold the mortgage. If the company continued making a profit at its current pace, the monthly payments would be made with no trouble.

"I think we have a deal. We'll let our lawyers argue over the details, but I am more than thrilled to have you take the reins." Mr. Burns stood and extended a hand.

Evan rose and shook his hand, copying his firm grip.

* * *

On his way home he stopped at the bank. He needed a loan for the $25,000 down payment. Luckily, Mr. Spackman was available to see him.

Evan explained the situation.

"I'm sorry, Mr. Ward. Although you have an excellent repayment record, the bank cannot allow you to take on more debt at this time. You have a substantial mortgage payment each month. Even with a raise in your pay possible, I'm afraid the answer has to be no."

Somehow, I knew that would be the answer. "Thank you for your time," Evan said before leaving. As he made his way to his car, he felt hot and angry, not so much at the banker, but at his situation.

When he arrived home, he called his father. "Dad, are you still interested in helping me out with Burns-Claybourne?" He filled him in on the new development.

"Sure, son."

"It's happening, Dad."

"It sure is. Your mother and I are excited for you."

* * *

It took almost a month of negotiations, filings, and signings to complete the sale, but Evan was the proud new owner of Burns-Claybourne. Mr. Burns had taken Evan under his wing and spent two weeks having him shadow the running of the company, all the while paying him as if he were still working the line on the third shift so he would have income.

"I want this to be successful as much as you do, young man," Mr. Burns said on several occasions.

When Mr. Burns' official last day came, he made a big production on the factory floor by handing over the keys to Evan in front of everyone on the day shift. Lots of clapping and whistling ensued.

"One more thing," Mr. Burns said as he and Evan returned to the office, "this is now yours." He handed Evan a set of car keys and pointed out his office window toward a silver Chevrolet Impala. "It belongs to the company. One of the perks of being the owner."

"Wow. Thank you." Evan had it on his mind to get a second car for his family. Now he wouldn't have to. This was much better than what he would have purchased, and it was a beautiful car.

Evan was glad to be working a day schedule once again. Evenings could be for relaxing and winding down instead of preparing for a night of work, and he and Mary could have time together as a couple.

At dinner, he announced, "I have a big surprise for everyone."

"What, Daddy," Linda asked. The others joined in asking.

"I am going to take you to visit Daddy's new factory."

They piled into the car, three to each row seat of the station wagon, with Klint nestled between Evan and Mary in the front seat.

Evan parked next to the Silver Impala but said nothing about it.

The first stop was Evan's office. He explained that during the day several people work with him, but that they had gone home already.

He led the family to the supervisor's office on the second floor which had large windows overlooking the balcony to the factory floor below. The kids stood on the desk and chairs to get a better view of the people working, sparks flying, and conveyors moving.

When the supervisor returned through the balcony door, the kids were startled by the sudden increase in the volume of the clangs and hisses from below. Linda covered her ears and Alison clung to Mary. Klint and Greg seemed the most curious. Evan thought, I'll bring them by themselves another time.

Back out in the parking lot, Evan stopped the family in front of the Impala. Evan held up the car keys, grinning.

"Mary, we have a new car."

She looked at him, her eyebrows squinted. "What?"

He pointed to the Impala. "Company car. Now you'll have our car to use during the day. No more juggling."

"That is wonderful." She and the children walked around the car, looking in the windows. Evan followed, watching everyone's faces.

"I thought maybe Klint, Ted, and Greg would like to ride home in the new car with me. What do you say?"

He barely finished speaking when the three boys ran to the Impala's rear door, jumping up and down.

CHAPTER 7

Transitions

The first few months at the head of Burns-Claybourne were less stressful than Evan anticipated. Everyone kept their positions and orders were filled as usual and on time. All is good, thought Evan, but we can do better. He looked for ways to increase sales and worked closely with the sales department to do so.

"Mr. Ward, Clark Butler from sales is on line one," Paulene said over the intercom.

"Thanks, Paulene." Evan was delighted with Clark's initiative to find new clients. Maybe he has another big sale to report. "What's up, Clark?"

"Not good news I'm afraid. That order for 40 model D3-7s was just canceled. It seems they got a better deal for a similar desk from another supplier."

"What about their contract?"

"They were supposed to be sending the signed copy back, but they hadn't actually sent it yet. We didn't start production, so we don't have extra inventory to handle, at least."

"That's a blessing. Can you find out who they bought from? I'm curious."

"I'll try."

Evan hung up the phone. He leaned back in his chair and sighed. He was depending on that order for his employees' Christmas bonus. He hated the idea of dipping into the company savings again after the upgrades to the equipment he already approved. He needed a sizable account balance if he was ever going to attempt enlarging the building and expanding the company.

He already cut back on his projected total once to give his employees a well-deserved raise. To his thinking, that was important, especially since they made his tenure as owner manageable so far. Loyalty like that should be rewarded. He loosened his tie and returned to his paperwork, not ready to give up on his dream. If it's meant to be, it will happen.

* * *

Clark stopped by Evan's office, wiping a couple of crumbs from his tie before entering. He had been with the company for only three years, fresh out of college, and had a youthful energy that Evan found commendable. "I have some very exciting news, Mr. Ward. Remember the canceled order last month for D3-7s? Well, it's on again."

Evan motioned Clark to sit in the chair in front of his desk. "What? Why? What happened?"

"The desks they ordered from the other manufacturer arrived and they were terrible according to their purchasing agent. Poor quality, cheap materials, drawers stuck or falling off their tracks as soon as they were filled. Some desks weren't even level."

"Good grief. Well, I'm sure they will be happy with ours, Clark. Can we expedite the order?"

"Already checked. If you approve overtime, we can have them shipped by the end of the week." Clark's cherubic smile was all the guarantee Evan needed.

"Done. Thanks for taking the lead on this."

"It was my contact to begin with. I feel responsible."

"Not every possible sale pans out, Clark. But when one does, it makes the extra effort worthwhile. That's what helps a company grow."

Evan looked out his office window. *Grow. How can I expand the company? What new product can we offer that is in demand?*

Clark got up and turned to leave, but Evan stopped him. "Say, Clark. Have you had inquiries about office furniture products that we don't make? I'm thinking of starting a new product line. Not chairs, though. We have a good relationship with Chicago Chairworks supplying them. I don't want to mess that up."

Clark looked at the floor for a few moments, then looked at Evan. "I did have a couple of questions about matching shelving units."

"Shelving units? Interesting. I will look into that. We could sell matching sets."

After Clark left the office, Evan took a few quick notes, made sketches, and called his design guy, David

Francis. "Dave, I have an idea. Meet me at my office at two-thirty."

The meeting was fruitful. Within an hour, they had preliminary designs for three-shelf and five-shelf units–steel construction with polished wood tops made to order matching the desks. Evan's excitement was growing.

"And we could offer a reduced price for our previous desk buyers. They already know we have quality products."

David added, "What about getting a review from them as part of the deal?"

Evan laughed. "I like the way you think, David. How soon can you have the specs ready for the assembly line?"

"Two days should be enough, but prototype units should be built and checked before full production."

"Right you are, Dave." Evan could have kicked himself for overlooking that step. It made him realize just how new he was to the manufacturing world, even after nearly a year.

David continued. "We have plenty of oak and maple for tops, and we can use a few of the steel desk leg rods and sheet steel from the warehouse for the prototypes. We'll have to order more to begin full-scale production."

"Yes, and we'll get photos of the prototypes to make a brochure."

David smiled. "A new adventure for Burns-Claybourne, Mr. Ward. Thank you for keeping us in business."

"Moving forward, one desk at a time, as Mr. Burns used to say."

"And now one shelving unit at a time."

* * *

"Mr. Ward? Do you have a minute? The snack vendor, Tanner Peterson, would like a word."

Evan pressed the respond button on his phone. "Sure, Paulene, send him in." What could he want?

"Sorry to be a bother, Mr. Ward. I spoke to the floor supervisor, and he said to see you directly." The older heavy-set man stood in the doorway holding a well-worn ball cap in his hands.

Evan sensed the man was nervous about entering, so he stood and approached him, speaking softly. "What can I do for you?"

"Well." The man paused and inhaled. "It seems someone or more than one someone has been using steel punchouts in the snack machines instead of coins." He took a quarter-sized steel punchout from his pocket and held it up. "At first, it was an occasional punchout, which–haha– kids do sometimes, but now it's several dollars' worth every week when I refill the machines. I am losing money here."

"We can't have that. I know how much our employees depend on those snack machines."

"And I'd hate to remove them, but I may not have a choice."

"Let me look into it. I assure you we have no kids working here. Do you know how much you have lost to these punchouts, roughly?"

"I know exactly. Forty-three dollars and twenty-five cents. I keep good records."

"A smart businessman always does."

Evan put his hand on the man's shoulder and walked him to Paulene's desk. "Paulene, give our friend here fifty dollars from petty cash. There is no reason he should suffer the loss."

Paulene took fifty from a small safe in the wall and handed it to the man.

"Thank you, Mr. Ward," the man said. He nodded goodbye and left.

Evan turned to Paulene. "I dislike having to deal with things like this. Couldn't everyone just be honest?"

"That would be nice," Paulene responded.

Evan had Paulene type up a memo to be distributed to all employees on all shifts asking that the punchout situation be stopped. He was willing to let the culprit or culprits off as long as it stopped.

The vendor did not have a good report the following week. Time for Plan B. Evan borrowed the master vending machine key from the vendor. He enlisted the help of each shift's supervisor. They were to periodically check the vending machine cash boxes for steel punchouts and note which employees had been in the breakroom with the machines.

Two days later, Evan had three suspects. He called each one to his office separately.

Suspect One was a new employee, a young lady just out of high school. This was her first job.

"I only did it a few times. I was told everybody does it, and I did see others doing it." She had a look of panic in her eyes. Her hands were clenching and unclenching rapidly. Her cheeks were flushed and stood out almost as much as her red hair. "Please don't fire me. I need this job. I won't do it again."

"I'm holding you to that," Evan said. She seemed genuinely remorseful. "But I expect you to be an exceptional employee from now on. Only your best work is acceptable."

"Yes, sir. I will. Thank you."

It did not escape Evan that it felt like he was scolding one of his children for misbehaving. Maybe the vendor was onto something, *I do have children working here.* Evan escorted her to the door of his office as she repeated her thanks over and over.

Suspect Two was a long-time employee of the company, a few years older than Evan, a family man Evan knew from his time on the night shift. As with the young woman, he admitted he was part of the scam. "I'm sorry. I wasn't thinking. I'll pay it back. I'm so embarrassed. My wife will be mortified." Small beads of sweat appeared on his forehead. "And I'm not just saying this to keep my job. I really mean it. Since you took over the company from Mr. Burns, the atmosphere has changed for the better. Not that it was bad before. Mr. Burns was a great guy to work for, but most everyone I work with seems to be very happy working here."

"That's great to hear. This other matter doesn't have to go beyond my office, but I need two things. You said you'd make restitution, so that's number one. Number two, don't ever do it again. If there is a next time, there will be no next time, if you get my meaning."

"Yes, clearly." The man's eyes welled up.

"You may go."

Suspect Three, a tall and lean young man in jeans and a black tee shirt, sauntered into Evan's office and sat without waiting to be offered a seat. "You wanted to see me?" He scratched his stubbly face.

"Albert Norris, is it? You have been identified as one of the people using punchouts instead of quarters for the vending machines."

"Yeah, so? What's it to you? They are not your machines. Why do you care? It's not costing you anything."

"That is very true, but my employees represent the company, and Burns-Claybourne has a good reputation. We can't have employees stealing from business partners, can we?" Evan buzzed Paulene on the intercom. "Paulene, can you ask Mike to come up?" He turned back to Norris, who was scanning the office like he was looking for something to steal.

CHAPTER 7 - TRANSITIONS

"Mr. Norris, do you understand my point about all employees representing the company?"

Ignoring the question, Norris ranted on. "Those vending prices are a rip-off. That guy can afford the loss."

"You are paid enough to afford those prices. You could also choose not to purchase anything. Either way, stealing is not an option."

"You don't get it." Norris folded his arms across his chest which Evan took as a sign of defiance.

"I'm afraid I do. Unfortunately, I am going to have to let you go."

"You are firing me?" Norris unfolded his arms and leaned forward.

"Yes. Frankly, I need my employees to be trustworthy." For a brief moment as Evan watched him stand, he was afraid Norris would get physical. *I'm not ready for this.*

"This job was crap anyway." Norris said, staring Evan in the eyes before turning and storming out the office door. The security guard, Mike O'Reilly, who had been waiting by Paulene's desk, escorted him out of the building.

Evan took a deep breath. *I hope I don't have to do that very often.* He took a few large gulps of water from his glass.

* * *

Two weeks later, Evan had the first prototype of the five-shelf model moved to his office and the three-shelf model in the front office behind Paulene's reception desk. His desk was cleaned and neatened for photos of the products in use. He placed several manuals on the shelves and framed photos of his family on the maple top. He stood back while David snapped photos from several angles.

David continued with photos of the three-shelf unit near Paulene's desk.

"I'll send you the copy to go with the photos," David said. "Once you approve it, the printer said the brochures would be ready in a week."

"Great, I'll have Paulene get the receptionist addressing envelopes right away."

Paulene nodded. "Right away, Mr. Ward."

"And the sales team needs to be on the factory floor to see the new units being made so they are intimate with the product details and are ready to hit the ground running when they head out on the road. They only have a week before the sales convention in Chicago. I'll see if we can't increase our sales area. If not, we'll make it work."

In order to fill shelving orders, Evan would have to make use of all slack time on the lines and add line workers to the overnight shift. At least until I get the new addition on the building.

Knowing that meeting orders in a timely manner would be key to getting a new product off the ground, Evan called the company finance officer to set the wheels in motion for getting a business loan for the expansion.

Evan left his office for his weekly tour of the factory, a quick walk-through to greet employees and listen to suggestions or concerns. It never took very long, but it kept him connected to the workers in a way he had not felt himself as a line worker.

When he returned, Paulene stopped him at her desk. "Mr. Ward, your wife called while you were out. She said to call home as soon as possible."

"Did she say what about?" It was not like her to interrupt his work day unless it was very important.

"No."

Evan sat at his desk and dialed. "Mary, what's up?"

"It's your father. He's in the emergency room. Your mom called to let me know the ambulance took him. She thinks it's a heart attack."

"I'll go right now." Evan grabbed his coat. As he passed Paulene on his way out, he said. "Family emergency. Gotta go."

CHAPTER 8

Passing

E van arrived at the hospital to find his mother in the ER waiting room. Her hair was disheveled, and she was wearing her old house dress under her coat. It was obvious to Evan she had left home in a rush. Normally, she would make every effort to look her best when out of the house.

"Evan, I'm so glad you are here. They've taken him to surgery. We can do nothing but pray now." She dabbed her nose with a wadded tissue.

"Did they give you any information about what happened?" Evan sat next to her. "It was a heart attack, a pretty bad one I guess."

The two remained silent for a long time. A black and white television played across the waiting room. Evan strained to hear the low-volume dialog. It was a welcome distraction from the worst-case scenarios his mind kept imagining.

"I'd better call Mary," he said after a while.

"Of course. Give her my love," his mother said.

Evan found a bank of pay phone booths in the hall-way just outside the waiting room and let Mary know the situation.

"And, Mary, just tell the kids I'm not home from work yet. No sense worrying them."

"I agree and tell your dad we're praying for him."

The parade of soap operas that played on the television blurred into one as the hours went by. Nurses came and went, ushering families to see loved ones, but no one came for Evan and Marguerite.

The news was on when a nurse called out Marguerite's name. She motioned for them to accompany her. Marguerite introduced Evan, and the nurse continued, "The good news is your husband made it through the surgery without complications. He's been admitted and taken to his room. That is where we are headed now. He's still quite groggy from the anesthesia, but I'm sure he would love to see you both."

The unmistakable hospital smell reminded Evan of the births of his children. Happier events, for sure.

Even in the dim lighting of Ray's room, Evan could tell his father was sleeping. Marguerite stood next to the bed and took Ray's hand. When she did, Ray opened his eyes.

"Hey," he said with an attempt at a smile. "Quite a day, huh?"

"You just rest and get better," Marguerite replied, almost a command.

"Listen to Mom, Dad."

"I'm very tired," Ray said, closing his eyes. "Thank you for coming." With that, Ray was asleep. They stood, watching his slow steady breathing until a nurse came in and whispered, "The doctor would like to speak with you."

They followed her down the hall to a small office. The nameplate on the door read DR. JAMES PEARL.

Dr. Pearl motioned them to sit. "Mrs. Ward, your husband suffered a very severe heart attack. We were able to repair some of the damage, but he is still in very fragile condition. He's looking at quite an extended stay at the hospital. We may need to do additional surgery once he has recovered enough."

Evan saw the tears in his mother's eyes. He put his arm around her. It pained him to know there was nothing more he could do.

* * *

Evan left work a little early every day to spend time with his father at the hospital. He hoped to see improvement every day, but it seemed his father was the same, weak and tired. He stopped at the doctor's office down the hall on his way out one day.

"Dr. Pearl, My father doesn't seem to be improving. Should we be concerned?"

"Mr. Ward's heart is still very weak. We're keeping him on supplemental oxygen. There is also a bit of infection that we have begun treating."

None of that was information Evan wanted to hear.

"Would it be okay to have his grandchildren visit?" Evan asked.

"A very short visit would be fine. I'm sure seeing them would lift his spirits."

"Thank you. They have been asking about him."

Evan took another peek in on his father before he drove home to tell Mary.

When she met him at the door and he told her the kids could visit their grandfather, she did not seem as excited about it as he was. "Well, the older kids maybe, but not Linda or Alison. I think it would be too scary for them."

Evan had to agree. "The boys then. What about Hayde?"

"It's hard to know how she will handle it. I think with the boys there and the visit being short, she should be okay. If we go after school, I could get Jeana to watch the girls."

"Sounds like a good plan."

"I'll call her," Mary said, heading to the kitchen.

* * *

Mary held onto Hayde and Ted while Klint, Greg, and Marc walked close to Evan as they made their way to Ray's room. Before the visit, Evan and Mary had prepared the children with a description of what they would see, hear, and smell in the hospital. For Shannon's three, it was a reminder of their time there, only the ICU part would be new.

A nurse met them at the elevator when they reached the fifth floor. "My, what a lovely family. Follow me." As they walked, she continued, "Usually we only allow two or three visitors at a time, but we'll make an exception today since your visit will be short." They arrived at Ray's room. The top light was on, and Ray was sitting up, smiling, having pulled his oxygen mask below his chin.

"Hi, kids. I'm so glad you came to visit me."

One by one Evan led them to the edge of the bed so Ray could give each a hug. The kids looked around at the beeping machine with its blinking lights. Ray took the time to explain what the monitor did and what the mask and tube was for, answering every one of their questions with a smile.

"So inquisitive, aren't they?" he asked Evan and Mary. "Just beautiful."

Evan could tell that Ray was reaching his limit. He was wincing a little and catching his breath, though he tried to maintain a smile.

"Okay, kids, Grandpa has to rest now. Time to say goodbye."

"Thank you for bringing them, you two. Such beautiful children, so well-behaved."

"Our pleasure, Ray," Mary said, reaching down and giving him a quick hug. "We're praying for you."

* * *

Two days later, while Evan was preparing for a meeting with Wade Collins, Burns-Claybourne's financial officer, regarding funding for the building expansion, Paulene buzzed him on the intercom. "Your wife on line two."

"Hi, Mary. What is it?"

"Marguerite called from the hospital. She wants you there right now. She sounded frightened."

"On my way."

Evan put down the receiver and jumped up from his desk, grabbed his jacket and called out to Paulene as he hurried past her, "Cancel my meeting with Wade."

He arrived at the hospital minutes later and took the elevator to the fifth floor where his mother was waiting in Ray's room sitting in the dim light. Ray was not there, his bed was not there either. Evan walked over to his mother and knelt next to her.

"Mom, what's happened?"

"We were here watching TV and chatting when your father got an awful pain in his chest. He was clutching his gown and gasping. Then he lost consciousness. I called for the nurse and they rushed him to surgery, bed and all. I've been sitting here praying since. Thank you for being here."

"I wouldn't want to be anywhere else right now."

He reached out and took his mother's hands into his.

A few minutes later, Dr. Pearl, looking very somber, and a nurse entered the room.

Evan and Marguerite stood.

"Doctor?" Marguerite asked.

"I'm sorry, Mrs. Ward. We did all we could do."

Marguerite sat back in her chair.

"Thank you, doctor," Evan said. He felt numb. At the same time, his mind was whirling. I'm not ready for this.

The nurse pulled over a chair for Evan. He sat down and held his mother's hands again. Tears were streaming down her cheeks. He felt sad, but the tears did not come. He had to be strong for his mother.

"We'll give you a few minutes," Dr Pearl said. "I'll be in my office." He and the nurse retreated.

Evan and his mother sat in silence for a while. He realized the doctor was likely waiting to talk to them.

"Mom, I'll talk to the doctor if you want to stay here."

"Would you? I think I want to be alone for a bit."

"Sure." Evan met with Dr. Pearl and then another hospital staff member to make arrangements for the transfer of his father's body to a funeral home. It felt very matter-of-fact and impersonal, but Evan knew it would be difficult for anyone in that job if they were to get emotionally involved with every death.

He returned to his mother in Ray's room. "Everything necessary is taken care of."

"Thank you, Evan. Can we go now?"

"Yes, let me drive you home."

Evan helped his mother to stand and they walked toward the fifth-floor lobby. Once on the elevator, Marguerite stood silently, looking toward the floor.

Since they were alone, Evan asked, "Are you going to be okay, Mom?"

She wiped her nose with a tissue she had wadded in her hand. "I know this sounds strange, but I always knew I'd outlive your father. I've thought about how my life would change, I just didn't plan on it being so soon and so sudden. I'll manage."

"Not strange, Mom. Practical. Let's get you home. Mary and I can get your car later."

"Evan, you don't need to spoil me. Though you are a son to be proud of, in case I haven't told you lately."

Evan blushed. "Mom, you don't need to spoil me either."

They both laughed lightly as they exited the hospital—a little bright spot in the sadness.

* * *

The funeral was a somber affair. Ray always said he never wanted a fuss, so Marguerite insisted on a short and simple service. That suited Evan and Mary with seven young children in attendance. Evan wanted the older ones to understand the loss and the honoring of their grandfather and had prepared them for the ceremony. The younger ones would not remember much, if anything, but he and Mary gave into Marguerite's insistence that they not be left out.

"Children are the promise of the future. Having them all there gives me hope," Marguerite explained. "I know it might seem selfish of me, but I want the whole family there to celebrate Ray's life."

During the service, many mourners shed tears when friends and family spoke of Ray's kindness and generosity.

The ride home was very quiet. Greg cried a little into his hands. Marc tried to comfort him.

After the children had been tucked into their beds that evening, Mary and Evan sat at the kitchen table having the last two pieces of apple pie someone had baked for them after Ray's passing.

Mary looked to be in a contemplative mood, her serious face made Evan curious.

"Penny for your thoughts, Mary."

"Did you notice that Klint, Ted, and Hayde showed no emotion during the service or afterward? It's like they weren't sad at all that Ray died, even after all of the time he spent with them since they came to live with us."

"Now that you mention it. Wow. I wonder why that is. Maybe they are used to people leaving. After their dad and mom, Grandpa was just another. I can see why they wouldn't be too upset if it's something that happens and they have no control over it."

"That is sad. I wonder how they would feel if something happened to one of us."

"Now you are getting morbid, Mary."

"I suppose. I guess we just have to make sure to love them and hope for the best."

CHAPTER 9

Growing Pains

Much to Mary's delight, summertime had arrived with a new normal for Marguerite. She spent more time with her grandchildren. Now that Klint was nine, Greg and the twins were eight and Marc was almost seven, they were able to play without being constantly supervised, and with Marguerite willing to watch Linda and Alison many afternoons, Mary had more time to devote to her volunteer work.

With Evan's paycheck substantially increased, the Ward family was living comfortably, though Mary was still careful with money. Years of lean times taught her to be frugal, with all expenses justified. At the same time, she was generous to those in more need. Blessings were to be shared. If buying a cut of meat on sale meant she had extra cash, she would buy something for the homeless men that lived in tents by the highway overpass in town. Her go-to was peanut butter and jelly sandwiches. She would often put the girls to work helping make them, though she felt they were too young to help deliver them. She wasn't ready to explain the complexities of homelessness. Learning to be helpful to others was a good lesson in itself.

Marguerite came into the kitchen. "Mary, Hayde is standing on the porch looking inside. She seems to prefer being indoors with Alison and Linda rather than roughhousing with the boys, do you mind?"

"Not at all. I don't blame her one bit. Those four boys can be hard to take with their cops and robbers and fort building and whatever other crazy ideas they come up with."

"Just wait until they are all teenagers."

"I will handle that when the time comes. One day at a time, Marguerite. Actually, I'm hoping I will have some big strong helpers by then. I'll put their muscles to work volunteering. I'm planting the seeds now. They're helping with the library book sale next weekend."

Marguerite called Hayde in from the porch. "Do you want to be Grandma's helper today?"

Hayde nodded and came inside to the living room. Alison and Linda ran over to her and grabbed her arms, giggling and pulling her to their toys.

Mary watched her mother-in-law with the three girls. It occurred to her that for Marguerite, the children were always her grandchildren, but for Mary, her niece and nephews were now her own children. There were many days when Mary didn't think of them as Shannon's children.

When they began to call her Mom and Evan Dad, she knew things would be okay. She couldn't pinpoint exactly when that happened. Having heard Mom from her own children so often, other voices calling her Mom seemed to have come without notice. How could I have not been aware of that? Perhaps it's just as well, I might have overreacted.

When school began in September, Evan stayed home from work for an extra hour to help everyone get ready. Linda was starting her first day of kindergarten, wearing a new yellow dress and matching hair ribbon. Mary pinned an envelope containing her milk money to the hem of her dress.

Evan held Linda's hand as he walked her from the porch to the bus behind the others. "You're a big girl now. Have fun today."

She turned into her father's hug, then followed her brothers and Hayde up the bus steps. Evan waited until she waved at him from a window before retreating to the porch to Mary holding Alison.

Mary wiped a tear from her cheek. "The first day never gets easier. They all seem so big."

"That Klint seems to have had a growth spurt. He's taller than Greg now. I never thought that would happen. He's actually getting a little stocky."

"He's starting to look like your brother," Mary said.

"And he seems more sure of himself lately," Evan added.

"Evan, I think you have a lot to do with that. He looks up to you. They all do."

"The pressure is on," replied Evan, laughing. "I'll do my best."

"I don't doubt that ever." In her heart, she knew how much that was true. She smiled at him. I married the right man.

She let Alison down and held her hand. "Let's go see what your dolls are up to."

Evan followed them into the house, grabbed his briefcase, gave Mary a quick kiss, and left for work.

After a doll dance party, Mary and Alison sat on the sofa to read a picture book. Mary looked at the wall clock. I wonder how Linda's first day is going.

She needn't have worried. Linda came home talking non-stop about her new friends.

* * *

On Saturday morning a couple of weeks later, Mary sat on the porch enjoying the fall air and watching Alison, Linda, Ted, and Hayde playing in the first of the fallen leaves. She heard the front door open.

"It's not fair," Greg said, stomping out onto the porch and plopping himself on the bench.

"What's not fair?" Mary asked from her seat in the shade at the far end of the porch.

"My friend said he would let me help him with his paper route tomorrow and he would split the money he makes, but today he says I can't. I was supposed to get two dollars. Now I owe Hayde two dollars that I borrowed to buy Matchbox cars, but I don't have it."

"Have you talked to Hayde?"

"Yeah. She said she wants her two dollars back."

"I know your father is happy you wanted to earn your own money, and helping with your friend's paper route would be a good way to see if that's a job you want. I'm sorry it didn't work out. Maybe another time."

"His dad said I couldn't help until I turned ten."

"That is understandable. Your friend should have checked with his dad before he asked you. On the bright side, your friend thinks you're grown up and responsible if he asked you to help. Don't be mad at your friend."

"I'm not, really. I'm just . . ."

"Frustrated? That happens to everyone at times. Even to me. Even to your father."

"Dad gets frustrated?"

"Oh yes. Remember when we only had one car and we had to keep getting it repaired? That was frustrating. But it worked out eventually. It helps to have patience. I know having patience can be hard when you want a problem solved right away."

"Like getting two dollars?"

"Exactly. Any ideas?"

The conversation was interrupted when Marguerite drove up. She got out of her car and stopped by the flower bed, leaned over, and pulled a couple of weeds.

Mary laughed to herself. She can't help it. Weeds have no chance with Marguerite around.

"You don't look happy, Greg. What's the matter?" Marguerite asked as she walked up the porch steps. Greg recounted his newspaper story.

Marguerite sat down next to Greg and put her arm behind him, resting it on the back of the bench. She looked out into the street as she spoke.

"You know, when your dad was a young man, he borrowed money from one of his friends, seventy-five dollars I think it was, to buy a bike. It was a bright red Schwinn three-speed. Unfortunately, your dad only had the bike for a couple of months before it was stolen."

"Did he get it back?"

Marguerite shook her head. "No. The police were unsuccessful, and no one we knew ever saw anyone riding it around town."

"I would be so mad." Greg pounded his fists on his thighs then folded his arms across his chest.

"I'm sure your dad was. He still owed his friend about fifty dollars."

"Fifty dollars! What did he do?"

"He kept making the agreed upon payments until the bike loan was paid off."

"But he didn't have the bike."

"It wasn't his friend's fault that the bike was stolen. He made a promise to pay back the money he borrowed for the bike, and he kept his promise. That's the important thing. His friend was more important to him than a few dollars. And a promise is a promise."

"I see what you mean, Grandma."

"I was very proud of your father for doing that. And now that he is grown up, he still thinks the same way. People are more important than money, and a promise is a promise."

"I need to find a way to earn two dollars to pay Hayde back."

"We'll help you think of something. And maybe don't spend your money before you have a surefire way to pay it back."

Mary sat listening at the other end of the porch. It was a lesson for Greg that seemed to have more weight coming from Grandma than from herself or Evan.

CHAPTER 10

Life Lessons

Burns-Claybourne's profits had increased considerably after the completion of the factory expansion and purchase of robotic welders. Evan was aware that the job he had when first employed by Burns-Claybourne was no longer relevant. He made sure the other welders were retrained for alternative positions. No one lost their job. In fact, the Burns-Claybourne workforce had grown by about thirty percent since Evan purchased the company. They were now one of the largest employers in the county.

Evan offered bonuses to employees who came to him with suggestions for better efficiency or money saving strategies. He knew the people doing the jobs were in the best position to know. Little improvements added up when multiplied by the large volume of products being shipped.

* * *

At home, the upcoming junior high dance was a big deal.

"Everyone at school is going," Klint pleaded. Being the oldest, he often took the lead when a parent needed persuading.

"I don't think everyone is going," Evan replied.

"Well, all of our friends are going, and most of the seventh and eighth graders I talked to are going."

Evan looked at Klint, Greg, Ted, and Hayde standing in front of his recliner. He smiled at the anticipation on their faces. They seemed so grown up all of a sudden, so tall and teenager-like. Klint even had a little fuzz on his upper lip. When did this happen?

Back to practical matters. "Do you have money for tickets?"

"We don't need money, Dad. Tickets are free if you didn't get in trouble for the whole marking period," Klint explained. The others nodded.

"Well, I'm proud of you all for not getting in trouble. But it's a dance. Don't you need dates?" Evan raised his eyebrows and grinned.

"I think you are messing with us, Dad," Klint said, squinting and looking Evan in the eyes. "We don't need dates. We just hang out and listen to music mostly, according to the older kids on the bus."

"That sounds about right," Evan said.

"So can we go?" asked Greg.

"Am I the taxi?" asked Evan.

"The best taxi there is."

Hayde spoke up. "Mom said I could go with my friend Kelly if you said it was okay. Her mom will pick me up and bring me home."

"That sounds like a good plan, Hayde."

Two days later, the three freshly-showered boys, dressed in their Sunday best with combed hair, piled into the back of the Impala.

When Evan picked them up after the dance, they were in good spirits, laughing and joking with each other.

"Dad," Greg said from the back seat, "Klint danced with four different girls."

"A popular guy, I guess."

Klint chimed in. "They just wanted to dance with someone taller than they are. I don't even like that last one, but I didn't want to hurt her feelings."

"Very gentlemanly of you, Klint. Thank you for that. What about you two? Did you have dance partners?"

"Yeah," said Greg. "A couple."

"Me too," added Ted. "I don't count the girls Hayde made me dance with."

"That was nice of you to do that, anyway, Ted. You are a kind brother."

Flashing red and white lights lit up the inside of the car.

"Dad, there is a police car behind us," Klint said, a little shake in his voice.

"I see him." Evan glanced down at his speedometer. Ouch. Over the speed limit by a lot. He pulled to the side of the road, rolled down his window, and reached in the glove compartment for his registration.

When the officer approached, Evan handed over his license and registration. "I'm sorry officer. I wasn't paying attention."

When the officer went back to his patrol car, Evan talked to the boys. "I was speeding. I'm probably going to get a ticket. The thing about driving is that you need to pay attention all of the time." Although he was embarrassed, he figured it was a good lesson for the boys.

"What does a ticket mean?"asked Ted.

"I'll have to pay a fine." He didn't mention the points on his license. "That is money I could have used for something better."

* * *

A few days later, Mary met Evan at the front door when he arrived from work. "I hate to hit you with this after a long day, but I think it would help if you'd talk to Ted. He's upstairs in his room, very upset."

"What's the matter?"

"He got in trouble at school. He wouldn't tell me."

Evan hung up his jacket and headed upstairs. He knocked on Ted's door. "Ted, Open up. We need to talk."

Ted opened the door, walked back to his bed, and sat.

"What's up, Ted? Your mother tells me you got in trouble at school."

"Yeah. These guys were smoking in the bathroom, and I was in there. When the teacher came in and asked who was smoking, I wouldn't rat on them, so I got in trouble for smoking just like everyone else in the bathroom. I wasn't even smoking."

"That is a dilemma. It sounds like either way you lose."

"I know. I hate it. I don't want to be a tattle-tale, but I don't want the principal to ban me from the next dance or whatever either. What should I do?" Ted used his sleeve to wipe the tears welling in his eyes.

Evan sat across from him on Klint's bed. "I can't tell you what to do. Your decision has to be something you can live with."

"We all have to see the principal tomorrow. I'm trying to think of what to say."

"Is everyone seeing the principal together?"

Ted shook his head. "No. I hear he wants to get everyone's story and see if they match up."

"So, no one but the principal will hear what you say. Remember what I've said before. Don't lie, don't steal, and don't be lazy. I think the first part applies here. If you tell the truth, you'll have a clear conscience. Some people might be unhappy, but they will respect you for it."

"Not sure about that at school."

"Think about this. What kind of man do you want to be? One who is afraid to speak up or one who is honest and trustworthy?"

Ted didn't answer right away. "I know you want me to say honest and trustworthy."

"Don't say it unless you believe it. Think about it." Evan stood and walked to the bedroom doorway. "And think about this, Ted. Is keeping the truth to yourself worth missing the next dance?"

Evan saw the flash of an answer in Ted's eyes.

* * *

At the factory, orders were increasing and shelving units were selling better than the desks, although desk sales had improved by almost twenty-five percent. Evan's workforce was now over 180 full-time employees and 20 part-timers. Evan sipped on a glass of water at his desk. *Can I call myself a success?* He could, but knew there was much more he could do. Now in his forties, he wanted to continue to grow for the next twenty years.

Paulene brought Evan a note from one of the employees. "Mr. Ward, here is a suggestion from one of the line workers."

Evan read the note.

Mr. Ward,

My suggestion is to order desk legs pre-cut to the appropriate lengths. I had the shift supervisor check on the cost to order them this way and with the amount we order, the cost would be minimal since they have to be cut in lengths to be shipped anyway. It would save time putting the desks together, and you would not be paying workers to cut the legs, so it would save money. Also, it would eliminate waste from errors and unused ends.

Sincerely, Robert Strain

Evan called the shift supervisor to confirm the details. Once he heard the facts, he decided to call the supplier himself to plan for the new orders. Moving the line workers from cutting to fabricating panels would save him from hiring more workers for the time being. *I wonder what else we are doing inefficiently because it's always been done that way?*

Though Evan was usually secretive about his generosity, he liked to make a big production when he gave an employee a bonus for a great suggestion. The following morning, he stood on the balcony overlooking the main shop floor where Robert and the other employees were arriving at their stations to start the shift.

"Attention everyone," he said over the loudspeaker. "Before we get started, I'd like to award Robert Strain with his bonus check for a great suggestion to improve efficiency here at Burns-Claybourne. Come on up, Robert."

There was a loud round of applause as Robert made his way up the metal steps to get his check. The bonus Evan gave Robert was larger than he had offered, and Robert gave Evan a vigorous handshake.

Paulene posted a notice on the break room bulletin board reminding workers on other shifts about bonuses available for efficiency suggestions.

Evan promised Klint and Greg that they could move their bedroom to the basement when they became teenagers on one condition, that they help remodel part of the basement into a livable space. They agreed. Their small upstairs bedroom was overcrowded with the four boys having grown so much over the years.

Evan taught them about framing walls, electrical wiring, insulating, walls and flooring. Not that he was an expert, but his own father had taught him enough.

"Well, boys. These skills might come in handy someday. You never know," Evan said after they had finished hanging the door on its frame.

"Can we move in today?" asked Greg.

"Furniture first."

The two boys ran up the stairs with Evan following. They would have to learn how to take apart a bed frame.

That evening, when the kids were all in their rooms, Mary and Evan settled into kitchen chairs to have a snack before bed.

"I'll be sore tomorrow," Evan admitted, "but it will be worth it to have happy teenagers."

Loud thumping and crashing noises came from upstairs, not the usual noise from children playing. Evan ran to see the cause. He bounded up the stairs and opened the boys room door. Ted had Marc pinned to the floor and was punching him, but Marc was blocking the blows with his arms. At twelve, Ted was two years older, but he and Marc were about the same size. Evan didn't have time to worry about who started it. He pulled Ted off Marc and sat him on his bed. "What's going on?"

Marc sat up, "We were arguing."

"It looked like more than that. Arguments are with words, not fists. You have more room in here than ever with Klint and Greg downstairs. Whatever problems you have, I expect you to work them out with words. Agreed?"

Both boys nodded. Evan turned, walked out of the room and closed the door.

"What was the problem?" Mary asked when Evan returned to the kitchen.

"I don't know, but I told them to figure it out on their own. With words."

"Will they?"

"I'm hoping they do. Without the older two there to keep the peace, they need to learn to manage themselves. I don't want them thinking it's okay to throw punches to solve problems when they get to be adults."

In the morning, Ted and Marc were the last two to walk into the kitchen for breakfast. Evan looked up from his toast and eggs.

Ted spoke first. "We're sorry, Dad. We talked it out like you said. We aren't mad at each other now."

"That is good news. I knew you two could do it. I'm very proud of you both."

"Do what? What were you fighting about?" Linda asked. "We heard you."

"Never mind," Mary scolded. "That's the boys' business."

Linda let out a dramatic sigh and poured herself some corn flakes.

* * *

On the way to work, Evan liked to listen to the news on local radio. It gave him ideas of places to donate anonymously to help his community. If the town baseball field was too muddy to play on, Evan made sure it was upgraded. If the Garden club was having a fundraiser for flowers on Main Street, they would find a generous donation in their box at the local market. If the county food pantry had run low, a truck full of groceries would appear. There was always someone in need, someone who could use a helping hand. Evan felt blessed to be able to be that hand.

One morning in particular, Evan was disturbed by news of a family of six who had lost all of their possessions when the moving truck carrying their belongings crashed and burned. The family did not have insurance and would have to start their new life here with nothing but what was donated to them to fill their empty apartment. A number was provided for people to call if they wished to help.

By the time Evan arrived at the factory, the phone number had left his head. He called the radio station, and they gave him the number to reach a local church office.

Evan called the church and introduced himself to the secretary. "Tell the family to go to Ellstrom's Furniture Store and pick out what they need. I will pay for it and have it delivered. I'll set it up with the store. I'll also have one of my associates bring them money for clothing and other items. I have one request, though. I don't want them to know who made this possible. This way they can feel good about all of their neighbors in their new town."

"Bless you, Mr. Ward."

"Remember, no one is to know."

CHAPTER 11

Selling

G reg ran into the living room jumping up and down, waving around his license, showing it to his brothers and sisters. "First try. I passed on my first try!"

"I'll bet I can pass on my first try, too," said Marc. "Wait till next year. Ted and I will both pass on our first try."

"Don't forget Hayde can take the test too, if she wants."

"Sorry, Hayde. Do you want to get your license?"

"Maybe." She went back to reading her book.

"Let's all get our permits at the same time. We can study together," said Marc.

"Good idea," Mary interjected. "You are all getting so grown up."

"We need to budget for more shaving cream," Evan joked.

Ted stood up. "You guys are forgetting one important thing. What good is a license without a car?"

"I've been thinking about that," said Evan. "Your mother is due for a new car. Instead of trading in the old one, we could keep it. We'll have to think of a fair way to decide who gets to drive it once we have several drivers."

Marc laughed. "I have an idea. Mom can get a new car every time someone gets their license. We'd all get cars."

"There are a couple of problems with that, young man. One buying that many cars takes a lot of money. Two, where would we park all of those cars?"

"We could pave our lawn," Marc offered.

"And what about the money problem? I might own a company, but right now that money is tied up in expansion investments, and I'm not giving myself a raise to buy you cars."

"We could get jobs," Greg offered.

"We are hiring at Burns-Claybourne," Evan said, glad the idea of getting a job was not his suggestion. "We take on a few high schoolers and work around their schedules. Education comes first, of course."

"When can I start?" asked Greg.

Evan laughed. "Your dad may own the company, but I still want you to interview and go through the process. It is a good learning experience."

Klint raised his hand. "It would take you years to earn enough for a car, and we'd need gas money and repair money even with a shared car."

"Don't forget insurance," Evan added.

"This is getting complicated," Greg moaned.

"Welcome to being a grown-up," Mary said. "It's not all fun."

* * *

A few weeks later, Evan hooked up a trailer to one of the company pick-up trucks to haul their dirt bikes out to the desert flats. Evan and Mary made it a point to spend time with each of the children one-on-one. This was Greg's day to spend with Evan. Dirt bikes were their recent hobby, and Greg seemed to have inherited Evan's love of speed.

After several hours of racing around on dirt bike trails at one of the parks a couple of hours away, they were tired, dirty, and sweaty. They decided to head home. Sunlight was fading and stars were starting to come out.

"Can I drive, Dad?"

"I'd rather you get some more daytime experience under your belt before we tackle night driving. Soon, but it's late and I just want to get home. We missed dinner, but I'm sure your mother will keep it warming for us."

Evan was flying down the highway, well over the speed limit, when a sheriff's patrol car passed in the opposite direction. Evan took his foot of the gas, keeping his eyes on his rearview mirror and saw the patrol car's brake lights flash on and the car make a U-turn.

Evan pulled over before the patrol car got close. "Quick, Greg, switch places with me." Evan slid across the bench seat and Greg climbed over him and sat behind the wheel. "If I get one more ticket, I lose my license. Just stay calm. Give him your license." Evan retrieved the registration from the glove compartment and handed it to Greg.

"Are we going to jail?" Greg asked.

"Just be cool. Don't worry."

The officer approached the driver's side and tapped on the window. Greg rolled it down.

"Do you know how fast you were going?" the officer asked.

"No."

"Almost ninety, young man." The officer looked at Evan. "You the father?"

"Yes."

"You let him drive like that?" The officer raised his eyebrows in a skeptical look.

"Didn't realize the speed, officer." That was the truth. Evan knew he had been speeding, but not sure how fast.

The officer filled out the ticket and sent them on their way. Greg drove for a few miles until they stopped for gas and switched places.

At home, they ate their late dinner. Greg showered and went to his room.

A few minutes later, Evan knocked on his door and Greg let him in.

"Greg, what I did was wrong. Tomorrow we're going to go to the justice of the peace and explain."

"You can't do that, Dad. We'll both go to jail."

"We are going to tell the truth. Even if it means I lose my license or worse."

"Do I have to go with you?"

"Yes. You're the one with the ticket."

The following morning, Evan and Greg arrived at a one-story brick building. A sign hung from a post on the lawn. William Duncan, Justice of the Peace. Before getting out of the car, Greg said, "Dad, I'm nervous."

"I am, too, but we need to do the right thing. Being nervous means you have a conscience and you know right from wrong."

The justice of the peace was an older, white-haired man dressed in a checked shirt and dark gray cardigan. "What can I do for you gentlemen?"

Evan handed him the ticket. "Yesterday, I was driving, speeding, and I got pulled over, but before the deputy got to our vehicle, I had my son switch places with me. I know it was wrong, and I'd like to make it right, whatever the consequences. I was a bad example to my son. I don't want him to think my behavior is acceptable."

The justice peered over his reading glasses and looked at Evan, then at Greg. "It seems you both have learned a valuable lesson today. Let's just let that be your consequences." The justice tore the ticket in half. "Good day, gentlemen."

Walking back to the car, Greg let out a big sigh. "I was so scared. I could feel myself sweating."

"But it worked out. The truth will set you free. I'm sorry I screwed up. Even dads aren't perfect." Evan tossed the car keys to Greg. "You'd better drive."

* * *

Clark, head of Burns-Claybourne's sales department stopped by Evan's office mid-morning as Evan was about to have a snack.]

"Yes, Clark, what can I help you with?"

"I got a call this morning asking if we have any desks for computers. Is that something we should look into? It sounds like a new market."

"It sure does. Let's look into it right away."

Evan had read about personal computers being in every business and every home in the near future. At the time, it sounded too fantastical, a magazine writer's dream. Now, it seemed real. This could be it. Desks for computers!

He and Clark met with Dave, of the design team, two days later. They shared everything they had found about personal computers.

"I didn't find any furniture companies advertising desks specifically for computers."

"Let's mock up some design prototypes and put together a brochure," Evan said. "Welcome to the 80s. The world is changing. We might as well take advantage of it." The excitement was evident in the higher pitch of his voice.

David was back at Evan's office three days later. "I had the team drop everything and focus on these new designs." He unrolled the stack of blueprints onto Evan's desk.

Evan examined each one as David spoke. "We studied everything we could find in print ads for personal computers for the home and office. We called computer sales agents and got specs for their popular models. If we make desktop monitor stands as well as full desk models, we could tap into the market of people who don't want to spend for a new desk. And they would be easy and inexpensive to produce, allowing for a high profit margin."

"Excellent work. And I am going to buy computers for our company. I've heard how efficient they make bookkeeping, inventory tracking, and payroll."

David added, "I spoke with sales about partnering with computer sales agents. If we could get them to recommend our products . . ."

"Always thinking ahead, Dave. I like that. We should buy a couple extra computers to use as models on our display. If people see how great they are, sales should boom. "

"That's going to cost us quite a lot, Mr. Ward," David said.

"Yes, but I don't want to cheap out on something that could be huge. It's a risk, but one I'm sure will pay off."

Evan sensed the worry on Dave's mind. "Dave, my philosophy is if you want success, you have to take it. You can't just hope it happens. Taking risks is part of the process. We'll invest in computers as a means to that end."

Evan was so excited about the new product line he joined the sales team at the next sales expo.

A steady stream of potential buyers stopped at the Burns-Claybourne booth. Evan greeted each one with a broad smile and friendly handshake.

Clark shook his head. "Mr. Ward, you put us to shame. You've sold more units in two hours than we did all morning."

Evan spoke to the whole team huddled around him. "Believe in the product and the customer will, too."

"I know, but somehow people believe you more. How do you do it?"

"I let the product make me look good, not the other way around. I'm always trying to live up to the product with my presentation. If I do, I make a sale more often than not."

"You've even sold to people that looked like they couldn't afford lunch, let alone one of our models."

"I don't prejudge anyone. If they stop here, they're a potential customer. In fact, I might try harder with them. If I assume they're not going to buy based on my prejudgment, I've already lost the sale before I begin."

"I see your point."

"You guys, the sales team, are the backbone of the company. If no one buys the products, what good is the rest of the operation? I have faith in your abilities just as much as I have faith in our products."

"Thank you, Mr. Ward," Clark said. He turned to the team. "Back to work. Let's sell, sell, sell. And remember what Mr. Ward always says, 'You can tell the customer anything as long as it's the truth.'"

Evan patted Clark on the shoulder. "Clark, I'm going to take a walk around, see if I can make some connections."

He made his way along the rows of sales booths. Every kind of gadget and gizmo seemed to be for sale. There was one thing Evan hoped to find. And there it was, a booth selling computers.

The young lady manning the booth smiled as Evan approached. She explained the different models and the software for sale that would help his business.

"Very helpful information. I'll take your card. Nice to have met you."

When he returned to the Burns-Claybourne booth, Clark and the team met him with big grins.

"Something good must have happened while I was gone. Spill it." The grins were infectious, and Evan was grinning even before he knew what it was about.

"Mr. Ward, you're not going to believe this, but Norwood Furniture, that big East Coast company with hundreds of showrooms, wants to carry our computer desks. If we can get sufficient numbers to their show-rooms, they will be included in their next big advertising campaign."

"Excellent work, team! Now I need to make a phone call. We need to up production starting today."

* * *

Over the next several months, orders were secured from two other furniture chains, one on the West Coast and one in the Southwest. To ease the crowded conditions of the main facility, a new building was built for manufacturing the computer desks, designed with optimal efficiency in mind. With the company's booming sales figures, securing a loan for the expansion was not a problem.

At a meeting in Evan's office, David congratulated him. "You were smart to buy up that vacant land down the road before you needed it."

"Well, if the sellers knew I needed it, the price would have been much higher. My goal has always been to grow the company. Having land is part of that goal."

"What if we have to grow even more?"

"I'm always on the lookout for a good deal. Even if it's across town."

CHAPTER 12

Integrity

E van stood looking out his office window, contemplating the new marketing campaign they were about to launch with several new computer magazines that had cropped up. The sun broke through the clouds and rays of sunlight beamed down onto the Burns-Claybourne sign in front of the main building. He didn't believe in omens, good or bad, but he chuckled at the coincidence. He had confidence he and his marketing team could mount another successful campaign. I think I'll suggest a sunbeam shining down on one of our desks for our advertisement image.

He was interrupted by a buzz from his secretary.

"Yes, Paulene?"

"Clark's here to see you."

"Send him in." Evan turned from the window as Clark opened the door and entered, closing the door behind him. That's unusual, thought Evan. Clark was running his fingers along the edge of a paper he was holding and shifting his weight. Evan noted his furrowed brow and lack of usual cheerfulness.

"I know that look, Clark. What's up?"

Clark stopped fidgeting with the paper and stroked his chin. "We have a bit of a problem that requires a decision on your part."

"Sounds a little ominous when you put it that way."

"Computer desk sales are booming, as you know, but so much so, that we are in danger of not meeting deadlines for delivery." Clark walked over to the window and showed Evan the paper.

Evan took the paper and scanned it. "I see."

"And I was hoping to get your permission to tell the employees to work on their birthday." Clark paused. "I know you usually let everyone have their birthday off, but it would solve a problem if they were to come in. We have three birthdays this week alone."

"It's a paid day off and something they look forward to. They always get the day off. That's one policy I won't change."

"Then we'll have to pay overtime for others to come in. That lowers our profits."

"You are right, Clark, and thank you for looking out for the company's bottom line. However, in the big picture, a few days of overtime is not that much. But if demand for those desks remains high, let's consider hiring another person or two."

"Will do." Clark nodded. "I will keep you posted."

"Oh, and Clark, you have a birthday coming up in a few weeks. Would you like me to tell you the week before that you'll have to work on your birthday?"

"Not really. I already have plans." Clark smiled. "I see your point."

"I thought you would." Evan gave Clark's shoulder a firm squeeze. "Everyone looks forward to their day off. And having your birthday off is a promise I made to every employee. Remember, build people and they will help build the company."

"But you know I would come in on my birthday if you really needed me."

"Yes, and I'd appreciate it, Clark, but I wouldn't ask you to."

After Clark left, Evan sat at his desk and looked toward the closed door. I truly am grateful for loyal employees like Clark. He returned to his marketing campaign planning.

Another buzz interrupted his thoughts.

"Yes, Paulene?"

"A Brent and Tiffany Smith here to see you. They don't have an appointment. Should I have them schedule one for later?"

"No, no, send them in."

Evan remembered when he first met the Smiths a couple of years prior. An older couple in financial trouble at the time, about to lose their home, had come to him offering to sell him their jewelry for $100,000. One look in their large jewelry box and he knew the contents were much more valuable than their request, at least ten times as much.

"Most of these were my wife's inheritance," Mr. Smith had explained. "Her father told her they were insurance for a rainy day. Well, Mr. Ward, today is our rainy day."

Evan recalled the diamond tennis bracelet, ruby earrings, gold chains, and necklaces, many with diamonds or other cut stones. Either they didn't know the value or were desperate enough to let it go for a fraction of its value.

Evan straightened his tie and stood.

Paulene opened the door and led the couple in, pulling a second chair from near the wall to position it in front of Evan's desk. Evan noticed the couple was dressed much more fashionably than the first time they met, Mr. Smith in a navy three-piece suit and his wife in a burgundy dress and matching shawl.

"Mr. and Mrs. Smith, how can I help you today?" Evan asked as he waved for them to sit as he sat himself. "It's been a while."

"Yes, a while," replied Brent Smith. "We took our jewelry to Mr. Logsden at Time Shop Jewelers as you recommended, and he immediately gave us the $100,000 that we needed, but he said he would sell the items on consignment."

"That was the suggestion I made to him. He's an honest man," Evan said. "I knew he would be fair. He always has been fair with my family."

"Well, imagine our surprise when the jewelry brought in nearly two and a half million dollars."

"Wow, that is incredible." Evan smiled, a little twinkle in his eye. "I'm so happy for you."

"So as a token of our appreciation, we'd like to give you a check for $100,000. If it wasn't for you, we would never have made out so well." Mr. Smith reached into his jacket breast pocket and pulled out a check and held it out for Evan.

Evan held up his hands. "I'm honored, but I couldn't accept that. All I did was point you to someone who could help you."

"And that changed our lives." Mr. Smith held the check forward again. Mrs. Smith raised her eyebrows in a silent expression of please.

"Tell you what, find a worthy charity you support and donate the money to them. That would make me very happy." Evan stood, walked around his desk to the Smiths, and held out his hand for Mr. Smith to shake. "It's been a pleasure hearing how well things have worked out for you."

"Bless you, Mr. Ward," said Mrs. Smith. She stood and hugged him. "You are a kind man." Evan could see tears welling in her eyes as he escorted the couple to the office door.

Once again, Evan tried to focus on the new advertising campaign.

CHAPTER 13

Fire!

P aulene brought Evan the latest issue of Rising Fortunes magazine, smiling as she set it on his desk.

"You all look so handsome, if you don't mind my saying so," Paulene said.

"Not at all," Evan replied, laughing as he looked at the cover photo. Evan, Dave, and Clark were posed in suits, standing beneath the Burns-Claybourne name on the front of the building. The feature article was of Burns-Claybourne now that the company had become a multi-million-dollar enterprise with more than 350 employees, including two of his now-adult children. Though the photographer wanted only Evan on the cover, Evan insisted his head designer and sales manager be included.

Reading the article, he thought back to the days when owning a company was just a faraway dream and how hard he worked to make that dream a reality. How sweet the success.

His team had grown, and responsibilities distributed to keep Burns-Claybourne an efficient enterprise. This place can almost run without me. That fact suited Evan fine. He had time to pursue his other interests;

racing dirt bikes with his sons, rebuilding classic cars, and taking Mary on sightseeing trips among them.

He never let the millionaire status he achieved make him feel elitist. He felt it was his obligation to share his blessing with others, financial and otherwise. One of his delights was to dress up in various costumes and perform for the residents of the local nursing home. One month it would be lederhosen and German folk songs, another it might be a Frank Sinatra impression. Sometimes he would talk Linda or Alison into joining him, especially around the holidays.

Mary asked him one day if he was considering retirement. The thought had not crossed his mind. I'm having too much fun. He knew at some point he would have to think seriously about it. Not today.

Evan looked out his office window. Beyond the parking lot, a row of mature maple trees lined the edge of a narrow strip of woodland, blocking the view of the highway. In the distance, a large plume of smoke rose above the tree line. That looks like it could be right in town, though Evan. That wouldn't be good.

He hung up the phone and turned on his radio. He looked at the paperwork on his desk, but he couldn't focus. He walked over to the window and watched the billowing smoke drift across the sky. The news came on. Most of downtown was being evacuated and several fire departments were on the scene. His phone buzzed.

"Yes, Paulene."

"Mr. Ward. Several employees are leaving. There is a fire downtown and they are afraid for their families."

"Of course, families first. Thank you for letting me know. And if you find out any employees have been affected, keep me informed."

Evan wondered if Linda was at work. The dress shop she worked at was right on Main Street. He called Mary, trying not to sound too worried.

"Just wanted to make sure all the kids are safe. You and Mom, too, of course."

"I tried calling Linda at the dress shop. She is working today. It just goes to a busy signal. She doesn't answer at her apartment either. Evan, I'm worried."

"Try to find out where people are being evacuated to and call there. I'll head downtown and see what I can find out."

"One of the church women, whose husband is a fireman, said they think it started in that new Italian restaurant. That's only two doors down from the dress shop."

"That restaurant isn't even open yet."

"Something with construction equipment during remodeling, I think. But the whole block has gone up and it's still spreading. Lots of apartments in those buildings."

"Maybe there is something we'll be able to do."

"I knew you would say that Evan. I was thinking it. Right now, a prayer would be good. I hope everyone is safe."

"I'll check in with you in a bit."

Evan gulped down the last of his glass of water and called out to his secretary. "Paulene, I'm going into town to see about my daughter. Hold down the fort, please."

"Yes Mr. Ward. I hope everything is alright."

"Me, too."

Evan paid no attention to the speed limit signs on his way into downtown. A burly fireman directed him to park in a grocery store parking lot a few blocks from the fire. Even at that distance, there was a distinct smell of acrid smoke. Evan walked toward the column of smoke as groups of people scurried past him away from the area.

He stopped a couple as they passed. "Excuse me, do you know where they are evacuating people to?"

"Most people left on their own, but some are at St. Peter's on Church Street," the young man said.

"Thanks." Evan crossed the street and over two blocks to Church Street and headed toward St. Peter's. He arrived minutes later and scanned the crowd on the sidewalk as they looked and pointed toward the fire. Flames could be seen above the trees. People gasped as something exploded, shooting flames even higher and adding plumes of black smoke to the gray.

No Linda.

He ran inside the church hall and walked quickly among the groups of people, scanning heads and faces. His heart was pounding. *I should have checked the hospital first.*

"Daddy?'

I know that voice! He turned to see Linda sitting with another young woman. She jumped up and ran to him.

Evan gave her a hug like he hadn't seen her in a year.

"I can't breathe, Dad," Linda joked.

He let her go. "I'm so glad you're alright. Your mother and I were worried."

"This is Ashley Nuckles, my coworker. We weren't even aware of the fire until someone ran into the shop and yelled for us to leave. We tried going out the back to our cars, but the whole back of the building was burning. When we ran out the front, the firemen were just arriving and they told us to head to St. Peter's, and here we are."

"Thank goodness," Ashley added. "If that guy hadn't warned us, who knows what would have happened to us."

"I don't think I'll have a car to go back to. Ashley either."

"Cars can be replaced," Evan said. "Don't worry about that. We'll fix you up."

"I'm more worried about not having a job," Ashley said.

"It just so happens we're hiring at Burns-Clay-bourne. It's not as fancy as a dress shop, but you could work for us as a temp for as long as you need."

"Do you mean it? This horrible day is getting better." She turned to Linda. "You are right. Your dad is a great guy."

Evan blushed and in mock surprise he said, "Linda, have you been talking about me again?"

They laughed.

"Come on you two, let's get you back to your homes. On the way, let's find a phone to call your mother. Ashley , is there someone you need to call?"

"Not right away but thank you."

There was a phone booth on the next block. Linda called her mother and reported back when she returned to the car. "Mom's calling Grandma and Alison."

Evan dropped Ashley and Linda off at their apartments about a mile from the center of town. Their buildings were only a block apart.

"You and Ashley could ride together and save gas money," Evan suggested as Linda got out of his car.

"We just might. If the shop ever opens up again."

"Think positive."

When Evan arrived home, Mary had the television news on.

"It's not good. One person is missing. Seven people are in the hospital. Fifteen families are homeless. They've lost everything. The fire is still burning."

Evan watched the screen showing firemen dousing the flames with water hoses, seeming to make little headway. "I'm going to call the mayor in the morning."

* * *

The mayor took Evan's call. "Yes, Mr. Ward. What can I do for you?"

Even ran his fingers along the edge of the framed family photo on his desk. "I was about to ask you the same. Is there anything I can help with? Financially, I mean, for the fire victims."

"I'm sure there is. I'm just glad no one was killed."

"What about the missing person?"

"Found. He was actually one of the volunteers who stepped up to help search until he discovered they were about to look for him. Lots of cheering and relief."

"I'll bet," Evan said. "Thank goodness."

The mayor continued. "As you know, those buildings were very old. Wooden. Not up to today's building standards. Apparently, insurance will not completely cover the rebuilding costs, so it looks like we're going to have a big eyesore in the middle of town for quite a while unless . . ."

Evan thought for a moment. "What if I give no interest loans to the buildings' owners to cover what insurance doesn't? Then they could rebuild right away. They could even upgrade."

"That would be a great help."

"One stipulation, though. When they rebuild, the displaced families get first dibs on moving in the new apartments. And at the same rent for at least two years. In the meantime, I'd like to make a donation to each of the displaced families. If it was distributed through your office, it could remain anonymous."

"Sounds good to me."

"Five thousand for each family should be enough to get what they need for now."

"More than generous," the mayor replied.

"I'll send the funds to your office."

After Evan hung up, he called the local florist and ordered bouquets to be delivered to the hospital for each of the fire victims.

* * *

Occasionally, Evan would go out of his way to drive through town to see the progress on the main street. Things were moving quickly and before long shops were starting to reopen. There seemed to be no shortage of customers returning to the area. Evan felt a sense of pride in his part.

When Evan arrived home from work one Friday, he gave Mary a kiss and announced, "Let's go out to dinner, Mary. And we'll bring my mom. There's a new place in town I'd like to try."

"I'll never turn down a dinner date," said Mary. "It'll only take me a minute to get ready."

"Good, because Mom is already waiting for us to pick her up."

They drove to Marguerite's and then to the new restaurant on Main Street.

"Wow! I hadn't been into this part of town since they finished rebuilding. It looks marvelous," Marguerite gushed.

"It looks like they added a floor or two to some of the buildings," Mary said. "It's nice that the facades were made to blend in with the older buildings across the street."

Evan parked, and the three walked to the restaurant, passing by the soon to reopen dress shop. When Evan opened the restaurant door, the smell of Italian spices rushed to greet them. Luigi, the owner, smiled broadly and crossed the dining room to welcome them.

"Dinner on the house for my special guests," Luigi insisted.

"I'm not having it, Luigi. We're paying customers helping you make a living."

"But you have helped so much already with the loan."

"Use my bill to help pay it back then." The two men laughed and shook hands.

When they were seated at a table, the best one according to Luigi, Evan said quietly to Mary and Marguerite, "Little does he know, I'm going to forgive those loans."

"Why didn't you just give them the money to begin with?" asked Marguerite.

"I wanted them to rebuild within their means, and I didn't know what their goals were. This way, each person set an achievable goal. Now, I can help them get there quicker. And no one got less or more than they needed."

CHAPTER 14

Moving On

Turning over the day-to-day operation of the company to his son Greg gave Evan more time to devote to his hobbies and philanthropic pursuits. He allowed himself the indulgence of buying classic cars, especially racing models, and restoring them. His latest acquisition was a deep red 1967 Camaro Z28 convertible. Even though he could afford the asking price, he was able to talk the price down. To Evan, that was part of the fun of collecting.

"She's a beauty, Dad," Greg said when he stopped by his father's garage which he specially built to work on and showcase his autos.

Patting the hood, Evan grinned. "She still needs a lot of work, but I'm glad you see her potential."

Greg stood his little boy on the driver's seat and let him hold on to the steering wheel. The toddler peered over the wheel, eyes ahead, looking ready to take off.

Evan laughed. "I might get her fixed up by the time Jeremy is ready to drive."

"Somehow I don't think you'd let a sixteen-year-old behind the wheel."

"Well, not if he inherited my love of racing."

"He may have. The reason I stopped by is, well, I know you talked a while ago about selling the company when you retired."

"Semi-seriously, why?"

"There is an interested buyer if you are willing to sell."

"As you know, it's been on my mind. But that depends on what will happen to the business. Not interested in anyone buying it to shut it down."

"No, this buyer assured me it would remain as is. I would remain in my position as would everyone else. The guy is very community-minded, just like we are."

"It sounds like you've talked to this guy quite a bit."

"I told him there was no point in getting you involved until I was satisfied with his goals for the company. I think he is a good fit. That is if you are willing to sell."

"I think I've reached that point. I did what I set out to do, run a successful business."

"And then some," Greg added.

"If it sounds good to you, let's move forward."

* * *

As usual, Marguerite had Sunday dinner with Evan and Mary.

As they sat at the table, Mary commented, "Strange, when I'm serving meatloaf, none of the kids seem to be available to join us."

"Coincidence, Mary," said Evan. "Your meatloaf is delicious."

"I agree," added Marguerite. "Their kids may be picky eaters and they don't want to hurt your feelings."

"Maybe I'll let them choose what I make for dinner."

Evan nodded. "Good idea, Mary."

Marguerite pulled a letter from her purse. "I got a letter from my sister yesterday. Her son, Scott, isn't doing well. He's in a nursing facility in Smithville."

"Wow. I'm surprised she even knows his whereabouts. Didn't he part on really bad terms?" Evan asked.

"He didn't contact her. The nursing facility did since she is his closest relative. After what he put the family through, I don't blame her for not wanting to be involved in his life now."

Mary looked at Marguerite and then Evan. "I don't think I ever heard either one of you mention Scott before."

"There really is nothing pleasant to say about him," Marguerite explained. "He left home at sixteen after causing all sorts of trouble for his family and was rarely heard from after that. Even then it was trying to get money for bail or something equally disturbing."

Evan added, "All I remember is the time we had the family party when I was twelve and he was fifteen. I told him he was being mean to the little kids, and he knocked me down, jumped on me, and pounded me with his fists until I apologized. Not a fond memory of Scott."

"There are not many of those for anybody," Marguerite said. 'The last I heard he was in jail for robbery, a jewelry store, I think. But that was several years ago. My sister said he has MS and emphysema and is mostly confined to bed."

"As mean as he was, I wouldn't wish that on anyone."

"I'm sure there are many that think he's reaping what he sowed," Marguerite said. "I know he put my sister through plenty."

"Has your sister visited Scott in the nursing home?" asked Mary.

"No. Just the thought of seeing him made her so anxious, she couldn't."

"Still," Evan mused, "I think I'll drive up to Smithville and pay him a visit. Maybe I'll gain a better memory of him than what I have now."

"You are an eternal optimist," said Marguerite, shaking her head.

* * *

Evan pulled into the Comfort Haven Nursing Home. It looked like a fairly new sprawling one-story brick building. Rows of large windows ran the length of each wing, and the grounds were meticulously landscaped. Evan couldn't help but wonder how Scott could afford to be there given the life he led.

The lobby had the feel of a hospital, similar to the local one where Evan often performed. Nurses passed by in their starched white uniforms and the smell of disinfectant hung in the air. A young receptionist gave him a visitor tag, told him the room number, and directed him down the east wing. He had not seen Scott in almost fifty years. His memory was of a tall muscular square-jawed teenager with a head of thick shoulder-length brown hair. When he entered Scott's room, the person in front of him was thin and gaunt, with wisps of short white hair and a few days of beard growth. The unmistakable jaw line was Evan's only evidence that this person was Scott.

"Hello, Scott," Evan began. "I'm your cousin, Evan. Marguerite's son."

Scott furrowed his brow and stared at Evan. Evan assumed he was trying to find something about his face that looked familiar.

"I don't blame you for not recognizing me. It's been a long time," Evan said.

Scott turned his head away and closed his eyes. Evan wasn't sure if he was being rejected or if Scott was just tired.

Evan sat in a chair and watched Scott who appeared to be asleep. After driving over an hour to get to the home, he didn't want to leave just yet, hoping to have more of an interaction.

A nurse stopped in and read Evan's tag. "Are you family?"

"Yes, Scott's cousin."

"Are you here to make arrangements?"

"Arrangements?"

"He is being released to the county home unless his family makes financial arrangements for him to stay or moves him to another private facility."

"I'm surprised he was able to pay to get in here in the first place."

"He's been here for a couple of months, but he no longer has the means to pay. I assume he had some funds saved up or a family member who is no longer willing to pay. I couldn't say. I only work here, but I know how expensive it is. Sometimes people who don't think they are going to live long, try to go out in style by getting into a private facility only to have the money run out before they go."

As far as Evan knew, Scott had no family willing to spend any money on him. He had heard rumors that the county home was overcrowded and was barely a step above being homeless. Scott deserves better. "Who do I speak to about this?"

"The financial office is near the entrance you came in."

"Thank you." Evan looked over at Scott and watched the slow rise and fall of his chest. Despite Scott's past, Evan felt compassion for his cousin in his condition.

Scott stirred and turned toward Evan. "You still here?" His voice was both gravelly and raspy, making it difficult to understand his speech.

"Yes. I came to visit you."

"Why?"

"Well, you're family. I came to see if there is anything you need."

"A new body would be nice." Scott coughed and wheezed, before settling back onto the bed.

Evan was glad Scott showed a little humor, but then realized Scott was serious. "I can't provide that, Scott, perhaps something more practical."

"They don't let in cigarettes, so maybe a burger, fries, and a Diet Coke." Scott tried to laugh but the phlegm in his throat caused him to cough and wheeze.

"I'll see what I can do."

Evan wanted the conversation to continue, but talking about himself would seem like bragging and he didn't want to know what Scott had been up to.

"I'll check on that burger." Evan left the room and walked to the lobby. He stopped by the financial office and set up a plan to pay for Scott's care so he could remain at Comfort Haven until Evan could secure a room at the local home.

Scott's nurse approved of the burger meal. Evan drove to a nearby McDonald's and returned to Scott's room with the prize.

"Thank you, sir," said Scott. "I was just thinking of this. How did you know?" He unwrapped the burger and took a huge bite.

Evan was caught off guard. It seemed that Scott had little memory of their earlier conversation or even who he was.

On his way out of the building, he stopped at the nurses' station.

"I noticed Scott has trouble remembering things."

"Some days are better than others," one of the nurses responded. Evan hoped for more detail, but the nurse station phone rang, and she turned away.

He left with the intent to return which he did almost weekly, enjoying the drive as much or more than the visit. Scott had only flashes of memory from his early life. Evan was often a stranger to him during the visits, but Evan continued. He would shave him and comb his hair, on occasion even helping him to eat. Eventually, Scott lost the ability to speak, but Evan continued to talk to him.

"How is my handsome cousin today?" Evan asked nearly every visit. He made it a goal to at least get one laugh or smile from Scott during a visit. At this point in his life, he deserves a little happiness.

When Marc came home for a visit, Evan persuaded him to go along to see Sam. At that point, Scott was too ill to even sit up in bed, but Evan introduced Marc and talked to him as usual.

On the drive home, Marc asked, "How do you do it, Dad? And why?"

"He's family. And he's alone. I have been blessed with good fortune. Not everybody is. I feel compelled to show compassion when and where I can. It's as simple as that. At this point in my life, this is important to me."

Marc was quiet for the rest of the trip home. Evan hoped he was considering their discussion.

When Scott passed away, Evan paid for the funeral, burial plot, and headstone.

Only Evan, Mary, and Marguerite attended the graveside funeral service. Marguerite told the others not to go out of their way to miss work or take the kids out of school.

"I couldn't convince his mother to come," Marguerite said. "Though she said to thank you, Evan, for looking after Scott at the end."

"I didn't want him to be alone," said Evan. "No one deserves that, especially when there is family nearby."

Mary leaned into Evan and gave him a side hug. "Even when he didn't know who you were, he knew someone cared. That is the important thing."

* * *

Greg oversaw the preparations for the sale of the company. He set up a meeting at the main factory between Evan and the buyer, Danny Tempkin. The two men chatted for a while and Evan was satisfied with the terms and the agreed-on price. A firm handshake sealed the deal.

Over the course of the next few months, while the sale was being finalized, the sales continued to grow.

Evan was at home finishing his leftover lasagna lunch one afternoon when the phone rang.

"Mr. Ward. This is Danny Tempkin."

"Good afternoon, what can I do for you?" Evan asked.

"I will get right to the point. I know we agreed on a price, but, Mr. Ward, the value of Burns-Claybourne has increased significantly in the past few months. I feel we should renegotiate. I don't want you to feel you've been taken advantage of."

"Danny, I won't hear of it. We agreed and the deal stands as it is."

"Are you sure?"

"Positive."

"Thank you. This means a great deal to me."

"And here's an idea. That extra money you'll have, share it with your employees. It will go a long way to ensure a smooth transition. I've always believed it's not the patents or the products or the buildings that are our most important assets. It's our people."

"Right you are, Mr. Ward. I can see why you've been so successful."

Evan hung up the phone and walked to the living room to join Mary. He felt a little lightheaded but passed it off as a reaction to his big lunch.

CHAPTER 15

Giving

O ver the next couple of months, Mary noticed that Evan seemed less active and energetic as he used to be. The shock of gray hair on his head was a reminder that they were getting older. She had to admit there were days when doing nothing but puttering around the house had appeal.

"What do we have on for today, Mary?" Evan asked as he walked into the kitchen for breakfast.

"Only one big decision to make. We have two young men in our ward congregation that are ready to serve missions, but they do not have the resources. They are trying to raise $20,000 by the end of next month."

"We should fund the whole trip for them. It's a great opportunity. Life changing."

"They've already raised about $6,000," Mary said.

"In that case, let's fund the difference, only make $5,000 from us and the balance from an anonymous donor." Evan laughed at his deception.

"You're too much." Mary joined his laughter. Not wanting accolades for his generosity was one of Evan's most endearing qualities.

Evan picked up the morning paper and scanned the lead article. He let out a big sigh.

"What's happening now?" Mary asked.

"The mayor is upset that the number of homeless has grown in the last few months."

"I haven't been helping out at the soup kitchen much lately. I would always tell people to try getting a job at Burns-Claybourne."

"And I hired a few, too. Even some with questionable pasts."

"Sometimes all they need is a chance to get back on their feet after making a mistake."

"Let me give Danny a call. I will strongly suggest he look into hiring from them. Maybe I can get him to continue the housing subsidies I give them as long as they stay on the job."

"That's asking a lot. He may not have the same values as we do."

"Danny seems very interested in understanding how my company became so successful and how it stays successful. This is part of the package. If he's too interested in short term profit, well, he may have to suffer. But I don't think so. Time will tell."

* * *

"Marc and the family are coming down for the weekend," Mary announced. "He called while you were out."

"I was thinking of giving him the dirt bikes. His boys are getting big enough to ride on their own. They'd love it. While they are here, We can go riding on the flats."

Marc, his wife and two boys arrived late Friday afternoon, just in time for Mary's meatloaf and mashed potatoes dinner. Mary was surprised when her grandsons requested it for their meal. Maybe it had grown on them.

"Denise and the boys and I have an announcement to make," Marc said. Everyone stopped eating. The boys giggled. Mary and Evan looked at each face.

"Don't tell me," Evan said, "you're buying a new house."

"Well, Dad, we might need to buy a bigger house."

The boys giggled some more.

Marc continued, "Denise is expecting. Twin girls this time."

"Congratulations," Evan and Mary shouted at the same time.

"Thank you. Feeling a little overwhelmed at the moment to be honest," Denise said. "Four seems like a lot, I don't know how you managed with seven."

"It will work out," Mary assured her, "and you have family to help whenever you need it."

"The boys promised to be helpful big brothers," Marc added. "Right boys?" They nodded. "But they draw the line at diaper duty."

"I don't blame them one bit," said Evan, "but that will change." He gave the boys a wink, to which they shook their heads vigorously.

Marc's boys were up early Saturday morning. Mary had their lunches packed and ready for the dirt bike adventure before Marc and Evan even had their breakfast.

Once the boys were on the road, Mary and Denise sat in the living room for a quiet conversation.

"I remember those days of rambunctious boys. They do grow up to be fine young men." Mary chuckled at her memories.

"I do hope so," Denise replied. "Marc is a good dad. They love him so."

"It doesn't mean they won't test him, though."

"Oh, I know that, but he's firm and fair. When they screw up, they know the consequences will match the crime."

"Marc sounds like he's learned from his father. And so it goes."

* * *

Mary woke early and decided to get up and get started on the lunches she needed to prepare for the homeless and needy families. What she started years ago with her family was now a community-based enterprise through the church. They served daily lunches year-round at the church hall and had added a food pantry. Evan was able to order foods at cost from his former employers at the grocery store ensuring that the foods given out were nutritious and healthy.

When Mary finished making the two-dozen peanut butter and jelly sandwiches, she glanced up at the clock. Evan should be up by now.

She returned to the bedroom and opened the curtains. "Wake up, sleepy head."

Evan didn't stir.

She sat on his side of the bed and gently shook his arm. Still, he didn't wake up. She shook harder, panic starting to set in. She could feel his warmth and could see his slow breathing, but clearly something was wrong.

She ran into the kitchen and called for the ambulance, and then Greg. Returning to the bedroom, she sat by Evan's side until she heard the ambulance arrive.

The two male attendants placed Evan on a stretcher while they asked Mary about Evan's medical history. Greg pulled into the driveway next to the ambulance.

"Mom, what happened?" he asked as he jumped from his car.

"I don't know. He won't wake up. Thank you for coming."

"We'll follow the ambulance to the hospital."

"Let me grab my purse."

The ambulance raced through the streets. Greg kept close behind even when the ambulance, sirens blaring, went through a red light. A few blocks from the hospital, the ambulance pulled over to the side of the street.

"What's happening?" Mary asked.

"We have to trust they know what they are doing," Greg assured her.

After a minute, the ambulance pulled back into traffic and finished the drive to the hospital, pulling into the

ER entrance. Greg parked nearby and walked with his mother to the walk-in entrance. Evan was nowhere to be seen.

"I'll handle it, Mom," Greg said. He walked to the counter and talked with the receptionist. Mary was thankful Greg was there. Her emotions were so near the surface, she was afraid to speak.

She kept her eyes on the doorway into the ER hallway. Every time the door swung open she took a deep breath. Nurses, orderlies, even a maintenance worker came through. She tried convincing herself not to get so worked up, but it did not work.

A doctor came out the door and walked over to the receptionist. Mary watched as the receptionist pointed toward her and Greg. The doctor started walking their way. Mary put a hand on Greg's leg to get his attention.

As the doctor came closer, he slowly shook his head. "I'm sorry."

CHAPTER 16

Legacy

H ayde was the last to arrive, the morning before the calling hours began.

"How was your flight?" Mary asked.

"You know Miami, delay after delay. I'm glad I made it."

"You're here now, that's what's important." Marguerite gave her a hug. "I wish you weren't so far away."

Hayde walked into the living room to join the other six. Mary watched from the doorway. Her heart swelled to have all seven children together. After getting a round of hugs and greetings from Greg, Marc, Alison, and Linda, Hayde squeezed herself between her brothers, Klint and Ted, who were sitting on the sofa.

She threw her arms around their necks and pulled them close. "I'm still the boss," she joked.

Mary turned back to the kitchen and spoke to Marguerite. "I'm so glad Shannon's three were able to come. They haven't stayed in touch much the past few years."

"Some kids are that way. They make their own way in the world. It's important to them to be self-reliant."

"Thank you for saying that, Marguerite. I sometimes wonder if they don't see me as their mother."

"You are their mother. Shannon may have given birth to them, but you raised them. You gave them a loving home. They know that, and I'm sure they love you in their own way."

"But they moved so far away. Klint in Iowa. Ted in Kansas."

"The boys have their own families now. They have jobs. They are doing well. Be happy for them."

"I am." Mary did not want to admit it, but without Evan, she would miss her children even more.

The viewing was well attended. A long line of mourners offered condolences first to Mary and Marguerite, then to the rest of the family. Mary's sadness came in waves. A humorous story followed by a tale of gratitude.

The funeral service followed at the church in anticipation of the large number of community members expected. By the time Mary and the family arrived to take their places in the front pews, the church was nearly full, with many mourners standing in the back. Many faces Mary recognized but many more that she didn't. She was overwhelmed by the kindness of the community she loved.

As the service proceeded, Mary was lost in her thoughts and only half paid attention. When the congregation sang "God Be With You Til We Meet Again," she smiled. It was Evan's favorite hymn.

Mary and the rest of the family were ushered out of the church behind the pallbearers who gently placed the black walnut casket into the hearse.

The driver of the polished black town car behind the hearse opened the passenger door and motioned for Greg to sit. Mary, Marguerite, and Greg's wife, Gretchen, were directed to the back seat.

Mary watched the hearse pull out onto the road as the police officer waved the procession to follow. There was so much to think about, but Mary thought only about Evan and the unfinished projects he had begun. Life changes so quickly.

The words of the bishop at the graveside were comforting and brief. Mary was glad of that. She didn't want to make a spectacle of herself crying in front of everyone. She preferred to grieve in private.

She walked carefully across the cemetery lawn holding onto Greg's arm. She worried that the damp grass would be slippery.

As she was about to get into the car, Marc walked up. "Mom, we'll see you back at the house."

"Okay. If you get there first, would you start setting out the food? There are so many dishes people have brought. I want it eaten. I'd hate for it to spoil."

"Mom don't worry. My boys will make good work of it."

"Tell them not to let me down." Mary smiled and thought, Life does go on. Mary sat in the passenger seat with the window rolled down. A few well-wishers stopped to offer their condolences once more.

As the group dissipated a disheveled, unshaven man holding a tattered hat in his hands took a step forward, then hesitated. Mary smiled at him as he approached.

"You don't know me, but I wanted to say what a nice man your husband was."

"Thank you. What a kind thing to say."

"Mr. Ward paid for my room for two months during the cold weather last year so I would have a warm place to stay. It meant the world to me. And it was big enough that I was able to let two of my friends share it with me for a while."

"It sounds like you're a kind man yourself."

"I do what I can, ma'am. I just thought you should know."

"Thank you for sharing that."

The man nodded and walked away toward the back of the cemetery. Mary watched him until he was obscured by the trees. She was touched by the thought of Evan being so generous and not even mentioning it to her. How many times did he do this? I wonder.

By the time the driver of the town car dropped Mary, Marguerite, Greg, and Gretchen at Mary's house, cars filled the driveway, and several were parked on the lawn.

"We never did pave the lawn," Greg said, laughing. "Maybe we should have."

They were greeted by many close friends and family. Mary was especially happy to see the grandchildren in good spirits. The last thing she wanted was for everyone to be glum.

"I'm so glad for everyone being here. Evan was a cheerful guy and wouldn't want anyone to be sad. Let's celebrate his life by being happy and enjoying each other's company." Mary made her way from room to room, getting and giving a generous number of hugs. Even though she missed Evan terribly, she felt the warmth of her family and friends. This is what sustains us.

After the get-together, when evening had arrived, Marguerite, Mary, and all seven grown children sat together in the dimly lit living room. There was a peacefulness in the silence.

Greg broke the quiet. "We should do something to honor Dad's generous spirit. I was thinking we could start a foundation that would help people in need. We could call it the Evan Ward Foundation."

"What a great idea, Greg," Mary said.

"But Mom," Linda interjected, "you do a lot of charity work, too. Maybe we should call it the Evan and Mary Ward Foundation."

"I second that, Linda," said Alison. "Mom and Dad both have such giving hearts. We should honor them both. What do you think, Mom?"

"Well, it feels a little selfish to put my name on it. After all, you kids certainly do your share of charity work. You have since you were little."

Marc sat forward in his chair. "Then why don't we call it The Ward Family Foundation? We could all be on the board to decide who to help."

"I don't need to be on the board," Hayde said. "I'll leave it to you guys. I couldn't say no to anyone. The foundation would be broke in a month."

"We wouldn't let that happen," Marc said.

"But I would feel guilty. I'd rather not."

"You have a good heart, Hayde," Mary said, "but I respect your feelings."

Greg looked around the room. "Any objections?" Everyone was shaking their heads. "The Ward Family Foundation it is. I'll look into setting it up next week."

"Your father would be so proud of you all," Marguerite said.

"I think he is proud, even now," Mary added.

The room grew silent again. Mary looked at each of her children and thought how Evan's generous spirit had taken hold in each of them. She took a slow deep breath and placed a hand over her heart. "So many people have been blessed by your father's love."

About Doug Wing

Doug Wing has over forty years of experience in manufacturing, operations, sales, sales leadership, and executive management. He was a co-owner and vice chairman at Little Giant Ladder Systems before retiring in 2019.

Doug was a member of the senior management team that helped grow Little Giant to more than $200 million per year in sales revenue; making Little Giant Ladders the 3rd largest ladder company in the world.

In the last five years of his career with Little Giant, Doug oversaw the cable and telecom industry, and was responsible for more than $150 million in sales revenue.

He worked at Little Giant for forty-five years with his father and other family members.

In 2020, he co-founded Boar First Investment Group. Boar's businesses include multi-family real estate, hotels, and property management.

In 2022, he published two books, *Giant Success* and *The Giver*. Both books were number one best sellers on Amazon.

Doug is actively involved with the Honoring Heroes Foundation, a charitable organization that helps fallen police officers and their families. He is also involved in American Indian Services.

He has served two missions for The Church of Jesus Christ of Latter-Day Saints.

Doug enjoys riding motorcycles, playing golf, reading, and fitness. He also enjoys collecting cars and motorcycles. He was born in Schwaigern, Germany, and lives in Phoenix, Arizona. He is married to Hayde Baladjay (pronounced Heidi Baladhi) from the Philippines.

Find me at
dougwing.com

Don't forget to leave a review on Amazon. This story is special to me and I want to make a difference in your life by sharing one man's story of how he found new ways to find new meaning for his life, his family, his community and his business.

Every step I took as a child in Germany, surrounded by family, brought me closer to the dream of success. These moments laid the foundation for everything that followed.

From humble beginnings to new heights, growing up in Germany with family by my side. The journey to success started here, with love, support, and countless memories that shaped who I am today.

www.ingramcontent.com/pod-product-compliance
Lightning Source LLC
Chambersburg PA
CBHW051424090426
42737CB00014B/2814